Please Give Generously!

Please Give Generously!

A GUIDE TO FUND RAISING

Anthony Swainson
with Linda Zeff

A GRAHAM TARRANT BOOK

DAVID & CHARLES
Newton Abbot London North Pomfret (Vt)

British Library Cataloguing in Publication Data

Swainson, Anthony
   Please give generously! : a guide to
   fund-raising. — (A Graham Tarrant book).
   1. Fund raising   2. Charities — Finance
   I. Title   II. Zeff, Linda
   361.7'632   HV41

   ISBN 0–7153–8929–7

Photoset by Northern Phototypesetting Co, Bolton
and printed in Great Britain
by Billing & Sons, Worcester.
for David & Charles Publishers plc
Brunel House, Newton Abbot, Devon

Published in the United States of America
by David & Charles Inc
North Pomfret, Vermont 05053, USA

Contents

To my wife, Délia
A.S.

To Colin
L.Z.

Foreword

When it comes to giving generously, the British take a lot of beating. Last year, donations to charities topped a staggering £1.4 billion with, according to the statistics, 90 per cent of adults dipping deep into their pockets in response to one appeal or another – that's around £70 for every family in the land. And of course the world of commerce, in all its shining manifestations, and other venerable institutions did their bit too. Well done, lads.

With so much generosity about, and so many worthwhile causes in need of support, it's not surprising that competition between fund-raising organisations is pretty intense – and growing more so by the minute. Everyone wants a slice of the cake, as big a slice as they can get their hands on. Fund-raisers have to be alert to every opportunity. The traditional raffle ticket, collection box and jumble sale can still play a part, but they are seldom enough on their own these days. Like it or not, fund-raising has become a marketing and promotional activity in its own right; so the more professional your approach, the more likely you are to succeed.

No one knows this better than Tony Swainson. In the fifteen years that he has been at the helm, The Lord's Taverners has been transformed from a happy-go-lucky group of kind-hearted enthusiasts into a thoroughly professional organisation dedicated to achieving a clearly defined set of charitable objectives.

In my two-year stint as President of the Taverners I worked very closely with 'The Captain', as he is known to all and sundry. Together we launched the highly successful Covenant Scheme, which today brings in a handsome £100,000 a year towards the purchase of 'NEW HORIZON' mini-buses for the physically and mentally handicapped. We even launched ourselves on the unsuspecting populations of Jersey and Monte Carlo – who may never forgive us – in our efforts to raise money for The Cause. And well worthwhile it was, too. Wherever we were and whatever we were doing, The Captain always made sure that we stayed on course and achieved our objectives, like the good ex-naval man he is. His energy, enthusiasm and inspiration seem inexhaustible, even at the end of the longest day.

Now, together with Linda Zeff, Tony Swainson gives others the benefit of his hard-earned experience in this very comprehensive guide to fund-raising. The book is packed full of good money-making ideas, sound advice and essential information for fund-raisers large and small. All of which means you'll have no excuse now for not getting the money in!

Good luck.

1 · Starting Off

Charity begins ... on the train from Skelmersdale

'Can I give you one piece of advice, Gentlemen: don't go and work for charity,' said the Director of Studies on the London Polytechnic's business management course.

He was well qualified to offer advice, but I was hardly qualified to take it. After being retired from the Navy, I was a 'new boy' on the job market at the ripe old age of fifty and totally unprepared for working in industry or commerce.

I'd taken the course to learn about a whole new world and, as it happened, to learn a whole new language too. I'd never heard of the word 'deal', for instance, except when related to playing cards: now I kept hearing people say 'Let's do a deal', and I was totally baffled.

Remember, serving in the Royal Navy you were provided for from the cradle to the grave. The need for a commercial sense and understanding of economics did not come into it. At the beginning of the month the paymaster gave you a modest wad of notes, and at the end of the month you were broke.

The money was always there, regardless of performance. In civvy street you're on your own.

It wasn't surprising, therefore, that I was rejected for job after job — although, at the time, I couldn't understand why nobody wanted me — and I became increasingly worried about my future.

Then, on the train back from Skelmersdale New Town, where I'd gone for an interview, I bought a copy of *The Times* and noticed on the back page an advertisement for an administrative secretary for The Lord's Taverners. It was rather pompous, but it did say 'suitable for recently retired senior officer.' It also said, to my delight, 'Must have a love of sport, and in particular cricket.' I knew I had to apply quickly.

That, in a nutshell, is how I took over the running of The Lord's Taverners.

The early years

The Lord's Taverners were just ticking along when I first joined, in March 1972. The only fund-raising events they held in those days were a spring lunch at the Café Royal, a Christmas lunch, an annual ball, a series of charity cricket matches in the summer, and the Harry Secombe Golf Classic. That was it, and we raised £18,000 in 1972.

The Lord's Taverners had been going since 1950, and in the first twenty-one years had raised £210,000, which is unspectacular but constant. Once I'd re-examined the system, we were pulling in that sort of figure within five years.

I achieved it with a lot of co-operation from the members, and better organisation. I didn't import expensive staff or equipment, it was just a matter of putting one's finger on the points which needed gingering up, motivating all our members to work for us, introducing many more events and things to do.

I soon discovered, too, that 85 per cent of our members lived in the south-east, all in the Greater London area. We weren't a national charity after all. So I persuaded the Taverners that we needed to have 'regions' around the country.

First, though, we needed to recruit people to run them. So we started a scheme called 'The Friends of The Lord's Taverners', which enabled virtually anyone to join – you paid your ten quid a year and got a Taverners' necktie.

These chaps went out and recruited their friends and business acquaintances, and we built up a network of fund-raising cells. Today, we have eighteen regions nation-wide and operate from London with a full-time staff of four and an accountant.

We actually hand over 82p in the £ to charitable causes – which, believe me, is a high percentage in charity terms. In 1986 we raised well in excess of £800,000.

If business overheads could be contained at 18 per cent there would be an economic miracle!

Our charitable objectives

Since those early days, when our showbiz members decided to put money back into youth cricket, our charitable objectives have been expanded to include:

1) the provision of equipment, artificial pitches and the running of competitive games for young schoolboys (The Lord's Taverners sponsors the largest cricket competition in the world, involving no fewer than 1,500 schools);

2) a contribution towards the provision of much-needed hard-surface playing areas in urban districts such as Brixton and Toxteth – in other words, adventure playgrounds, which are quite expensive to construct as well as involving the permanent running costs of a play leader;

3) the provision of 'NEW HORIZON' mini-buses for the mentally and physically handicapped. At the time of writing we put one on the road every eight working days. The cost of one of these specially equipped buses is around £16,000 so, as you can see, it is a heavy financial burden to maintain the striking rate;

4) special projects, such as the provision of a range of sports facilities for the mentally and physically handicapped. Did you know, for example, that there are blind cricketers and one-armed golfers? One is full of admiration for people with such courage and perseverence, who refuse to let their handicaps stop them enjoying life to the full – in fact, I recently read of a blind golfer who scored a hole in one. Amazing!

My charity philosophy

To be honest, the great attraction to me of working for charity is *not* the feeling of doing good – although I do get enormous satisfaction when we give money away to deserving causes – but of running a successful show. I have an overwhelming feeling of responsibility, I can be creative, and – within limits – do what I like to raise funds.

At the beginning, I hadn't a clue how to run a charity, or indeed any organisation – I just applied naval management principles. I knew how to get the best out of people, how to motivate them.

And that's what charity work is all about.

You *have* to have energy and enthusiasm or your charity will fall flat on its face. I've always managed to be ridiculously enthusiastic about everything I've done for the Taverners – it's the only way to inspire people. After all, like many charity workers, they're doing the unglamorous job of backroom boy volunteer worker.

I go in and have a laugh and a joke with them, I bring my secretary flowers every week. . . . That's because I believe my staff are absolutely crucial and important people, and it's one of the tangible ways I can show them how much I appreciate them and their efforts.

A job fit for a prince

The Lord's Taverners was founded in 1950 by a team of actors and well-known people – Ian Carmichael, Laurence Olivier, John Snagge, Jack Payne and Martin Boddey among them – who used to watch cricket outside the tavern at Lord's with a pint in their hands. They decided to put something back into the game for all the fun they'd had out of watching it in the days when Edrich and Compton were weaving their magic spell for Middlesex and England.

One of their number was a naval captain called Jackie Broome – the author of a book about the convoy disaster, the PQ17 – who had once served on a ship with Prince Philip. He took it upon himself to trot down to Clarence House and invite the Prince to be President of their newly-formed Lord's Taverners charity.

The apocryphal account went thus:

'No, I'm far too busy,' replied the husband of the then Princess Elizabeth.

'Then what about being the Twelfth Man?' (The Twelfth Man, in cricket, carries the drinks out to the chaps, carries the bag from the station and is general stooge.)

'Yes, that suits me fine. I'll be Patron,' he agreed.

Prince Philip has been Patron and Twelfth Man ever since – and an inspiration to us all.

2 · Rules and Regulations

What is a charity?

Charity means different things to different people, but undeniably charity means love – giving help and succour where it is needed. The mainspring of charity is an altruistic impulse to give money and service for the relief of the deprived and to improve the quality of life for the community.

Charity in England is as old as the hills, though much of what was once the domain of charity workers has now been taken over by the State. In the *1601 Statute of Charitable Uses* the list of charitable objectives included the relief of aged and poor people; the maintenance of the sick, soldiers, sailors and other schools of learning; and the education and care of orphans, while the first real classification of charity objects based upon law was made in 1891 with the following declaration:

Charity in its legal sense comprises principle divisions: (i) trusts for the relief of poverty (ii) trusts for the advancement of education (iii) trusts for the advancement of religion and (iv) trusts for other purposes beneficial to the community.

Poverty, education, religion and a benefit to the community have since formed the basis of all charitable activity and its legal interpretation.

Start as you mean to go on

Whatever the aims of your fund-raising organisation, you must start by setting it up formally and legally. This is specially important if you plan to get any kind of financial help; in addition, remember

that the more guidelines you have in writing, the less chance of disagreements among members in the long run.

Potential contributors will also want to be sure that your organisation is run correctly and profitably, and that the funds will be disbursed sensibly.

Fund-raising is fun

Before you embark on any kind of fund-raising, it is also important to remember that it must be fun. While your objectives will always be compelling and serious, the methods you employ to achieve your target should enable all involved to enjoy themselves.

The British public is, by nature, generous in its giving habits, but people will give more freely if you are cheerful in the way you go about your work.

Don't misunderstand me, though – fund-raising has its serious side: charity law will keep you on the straight and narrow much of the time, and you must be fully conversant with all the many rules and regulations surrounding fund-raising work.

But, having complied with the law, go out there and have fun. We all love a cheerful giver, so try to reciprocate! For example, when holding a fund-raising luncheon by all means have a speaker who will do the 'God-spot', the Billy Graham message if you like, but temper this with a comic speaker if you can.

Raise a laugh and you will succeed in raising the cash.

Choosing a name and aim

When I was in the Royal Navy, I was seconded to the Royal Air Force to attend their staff college, where we were taught all about the 'Aim or Objective and Factors Affecting the Aim'. Commerce and industry adopted the service teaching for business use – management by objective, it was called.

Basically, it is common sense. A ship must have a course to steer if it is to reach its destination. A charity, therefore, must have a well-charted course – ie charitable objectives – and a name that, where possible, reflects it.

Charitable objectives

The preparation and wording of charitable objectives need

careful handling and should be drawn up with the aid of a solicitor. Your objectives must be clear, credible and understood.

An excellent example is Cancer Research: everyone knows about the threat of cancer, everyone knows there is an urgent need for research. Cancer Research also has the other essential ingredient for success – it is *emotive*.

All registered charities in England and Wales have their objectives approved by the Charity Commissioners, who are responsible for seeing that they conform with charity law. (See Appendix – and for Scotland and Northern Ireland, page 22.)

But I feel the most important thing is to make sure that what a charity is trying to do is both appealing and acceptable to the British public. It is, after all, the public who will be the subscribers.

Two things to remember about charitable objectives

1) In commercial terms, the name of a product is most important. The same applies to a charity product. Too often, objectives are written in legalese for Memorandum and Articles of Association – ie the Constitution – rather than for public acceptance and understanding.

Another important reason for clearly-defined objectives is to be able to refuse, without embarrassment, numerous requests for grant-aid (ie the money you are able to give away). A polite letter explaining that such and such a request does not come within your charity's Memorandum and Articles of Association is better than making excuses.

2) Objectives should be able to flow easily from the name of the charity as much as possible, though it's not a bad thing to be a little flexible.

In my case, for example, The Lord's Taverners – as its name implies – is a cricketing charity. Our first charitable objective, therefore, is the support of youth cricket in all its aspects: competitions, coaching, provision of equipment and artificial pitches; while our second objective is the provision of adventure playgrounds, still very much in demand in the cause of serving young people and sport.

A few years ago, however, in order to ginger up the emotive appeal of our charity and to meet a very real need in the community, The Lord's Taverners introduced another charitable objective: a mini-bus for the mentally and physically handicapped.

We called the first one we gave away, ten years ago, a 'Mobile Playing Field', which appeared to have some connotation of sport. Now, though, we call the mini-buses 'NEW HORIZONS' because when handicapped children are taken out of the confines of home or hospital into the fresh air and wide world, it does literally open up new horizons for them.

(We changed to this name after a dear old boy, sitting in a wheelchair, looked up and said to me, 'Oh, this bus is marvellous. It's opened up new horizons for us.')

The inclusion of this third objective has enabled The Lord's Taverners to have a more emotive appeal amongst those who are not particularly sold on the idea of encouraging young people to play cricket.

The benefits of charitable status

In England and Wales, charitable status is conferred on a fund-raising body by the Charity Commissioners (see Appendix) provided a general charitable intent has been established. The principal benefit of this is exemption from most forms of direct taxation and rate relief (see page 51).

It's worth bearing in mind that many trusts and companies will only grant-aid (ie give money to) registered charities.

USEFUL BOOKLET: 'Charitable Status', obtainable from the Directory of Social Change, Radius Works, Back Lane, London NW3 1HL, which covers all aspects of registering a charity. At the time of writing this costs £4.95.

Drawing up your constitution

You will have to draw up a constitution (also known as Memorandum and Articles of Association) to submit to the Charity Commissioners (or relevant bodies outside England and Wales) for approval. They in turn will have to seek the approval of the Inland Revenue, who grant the tax concessions.

Your constitution is an important document, and I'd strongly advise getting legal help in drawing it up. Any solicitor is capable of doing this – and if he is versed in charity law, all to the good. Perhaps you've got a solicitor among your volunteers, who may offer his or her services free!

Your constitution will cover the following aspects:

1) *Charitable objectives.* This clause is the *raison d'être* of the charity. Remember that, above all, your organisation must exist for public benefit.

2) *Powers.* That is, the way the charity is to be run. This will deal with trustees, directors or management committees, who will form the governing body of the organisation. The scope of their authority must be defined, as well as how they are to be elected and discharged, and their powers of delegation.

The legal format of your charity (see below) will determine whether you have directors or trustees; you then decide on the powers largely on the basis of what you want to achieve.

The powers of a chairman need defining, for instance. You might decide that he should serve for no more than two years, or you might choose to elect a permanent chairman. You might also decide that no councillor or member of the governing body may serve for more than three years without being re-elected.

3) *Membership.* You must decide who are to be members and what their rights and duties will be.

4) *Investment of funds.* You must record how any surplus funds are to be dealt with. This subject, as well as those above, is covered in detail later in this book.

5) *Dissolution.* You must decide what will happen to any funds left if the organisation is wound up for any reason.

Choosing a legal format

The two main legal formats for an organisation are *a company limited by guarantee* and *a trust*. It is a matter of individual choice when deciding which to adopt because, as you'll see, each has both advantages and disadvantages.

(By the way, you don't have to adopt a legal format if your fund-raising venture is a one-off – for example, if you're a small group of friends raising money to pay for a specially adapted wheelchair for a local handicapped person. But you will have to talk to your bank manager about opening and administering a special bank account.)

A company limited by guarantee
This has no shareholders and cannot distribute any of its profits to members. Activities are regulated by the Companies Act and annual audits have to be made, which must be lodged at Companies House.

A company limited by guarantee is required to have members who elect officers. There is no liability on the directors should the charity get into debt except in the case of fraud. Nor can the charity be sued. The directors do, however, have to ensure that the funds are disbursed in accordance with your charitable objectives.

Advantages
A charity which is limited by guarantee has no claim on its directors except for fraudulent cases. That means that provided the funds are distributed in accordance with the constitution of the charity, there can be no legal liability.

Disadvantages
A limited company comes under the Companies Act and therefore has to have an annual audit and lodge the results of the audit with the Charity Commissioners.

A trust
A body of trustees are personally liable for the affairs of the trust. However, trusts do not have to be audited unless it is laid down in the constitution.

Advantages
It is easier to set up a charitable trust which is not limited by guarantee. It will require a set of constitutional rules but it is easier and cheaper to set up as no Memorandum and Articles of Association are needed, and trusts do not come under the Companies Act. Nor do they require annual audits.

Disadvantages
The trustees are totally responsible for financial losses. That means that they themselves can be sued for debts incurred by the trust.

Once you are registered . . .

The Charity Commissioners keep a record of all registered charities whose accounts are open to public scrutiny; there are currently 155,000 registered charities in the UK. When you are registered you will be given a number which should be displayed on all your correspondence.

Foreign bodies

In Scotland and Northern Ireland, there is no registration procedure:

In Scotland a prospective charity should submit its draft constitution to its local Inspector of Taxes, and the approved constitution to the Inland Revenue in Edinburgh.

Scottish organisations can get advice on charitable status from the Scottish Council of Social Service, 18 Claremont Crescent, Edinburgh EH7 4QD.

In Northern Ireland the prospective charity should deal direct with the Inland Revenue in Bootle.

Charities in Northern Ireland can get advice on charitable status from the Northern Ireland Department of Finance.

3 · The Workers

Working for charity

You'll get out of being involved with a fund-raising organisation what you put into it. That may sound very pious and platitudinous but it is nevertheless true. You can sit on the sidelines and come to all the functions, or you can actually get stuck in and fund-raise and therefore get more out of your commitment.

So it's not a question of what a charity will offer you, it's really what you can offer a charity.

Why do people join fund-raising organisations?

It's frightful to say it, but I'm afraid an awful lot of people join charities, in particular, for some recognition — not simply for personal satisfaction. They think if they work hard they'll get an OBE or something for their efforts. While at the management level charity work still has rather snobbish connotations — that's a throwback from Queen Victoria.

Many people see working for a charity — or, in fact, any fund-raising organisation — as a way of meeting people, too: The Lord's Taverners, for instance, is first and foremost a club. Others are motivated by a personal interest in the cause — perhaps following a personal tragedy of their own.

Whatever their motives, though, fund-raisers are invaluable, and the majority of voluntary workers are saints.

What about the workers?

There are two levels of charity worker. There's Lady Bountiful who says 'How terribly kind of you, Miss Jones. You've done a marvellous job tearing up all those bits of paper last week,' while she's been doing very little; and there's The Worker who pitches in with everything from addressing envelopes to standing outside the Tube station rattling a collecting box.

But they are both just as important – Lady Bountiful will have contacts and open all kinds of doors for you, if you use her talents correctly, while The Worker is the mainstay of any group, coping with all the detailed work.

So basically you need the worker category – the 'runner', the legs person – and you need the chap with the cheque book and the clout.

The 'passengers'

They're the people who do nothing – and, to make matters worse, tend to complain all the time! They'll tell you what a lousy table they had at your last event, that the food was awful, that the ticket price was too high. And you'll begin to wonder whether you actually need all the hassle. But you do!

You must swallow your pride and treat these people like valued clients – 'I'm so sorry you had a bad table,' and so forth. Because, infuriating as it may be, you need them – to take tables at your events, buy tickets at your concerts etc.

A case for kid gloves

If you're a charity organiser, you have to learn to handle the voluntary workers with kid gloves, especially if, like me, you're the 'professional'.

Volunteers will be drawn from all walks of life and are, of course, professionals in their own right – advertising executives, accountants, business men and women etc. And, strange as it may seem, many see fund-raising and charity work as a form of relaxation and do not always relish a too-professional approach from the director!

So admonishment for failure to 'deliver' has to be expounded with both tact and charm; you can't tell someone off for being late for a meeting, either.

It's the same with getting something done for nothing – printing, for example. If a printer is doing the job free of charge you're going to be at the bottom of the pile – first, he's going to service the companies who pay the bills. So it's no good phoning up the printer and saying, 'The copy date was last week – where are my invitation cards?'

Remember, too, that you must be very careful when appointing someone – to run a region, for example – because you can't get rid of a volunteer. We're not in the hire and fire business.

I have made the occasional mistake in this respect and it is highly embarrassing getting rid of someone unless he or she has absconded with the funds!

Facing the problems

1) Resentment

The voluntary worker is the guts of the charity or fund-raising organisation, and, believe it or not, many are very jealous of the professional – or the 'hired hack', if you like. Some volunteers really resent the charity spending money on paying someone to do the job professionally – 'Why is this person getting paid when I do all this work for nothing?' they're thinking. And you can't really blame them.

But what volunteers don't realise is that they're only responsible for one aspect of the charity, whereas for the director the co-ordination work is a full-time occupation which he or she would not have the time to do for free.

So a word or two to the director of any group: don't throw your weight around too much until you've found out where you stand with the voluntary worker. I've had letters of complaint to the chairman about my relationship with voluntary workers – 'Who does he think he is, giving orders?' type of approach. Back to wearing the kid gloves!

I have, however, made many good friends by working with my voluntary workers in The Lord's Taverners. Some of them have a dedication and work ethic beyond belief. They should all have OBEs!

On the whole, I'm glad to say, most people respect the professional. Without voluntary help, though, the organisation's work would not get done. So volunteers and professionals must try to develop a good working relationship with one another.

And if the professional is no good, sack him!

2) An unusual kind of company

You wouldn't expect the managing director of a company to make do with a staff of volunteers. But that's exactly what happens to the director of a charity.

I'm a managing director with four paid secretaries, but the people who are actually going to fund-raise with me are all part-time volunteers. You couldn't run a company like that! It leads to all kinds of problems, not least the fact that the director must tread very carefully. You can't go around saying, 'Why haven't you done this, or that?' Like all charity directors, I have to go cap in hand all the time to part-time volunteers and amateurs.

It's quite amazing that charities are competitive and make money, isn't it?

3) **Short change**

As well as the problem of dealing with amateurs, all charity managers must realise that they're dealing with people whose motivation and enthusiasm is not constant. So, very often, you have to renew the driving force of an aspect of your work.

Volunteers – and you can't blame them, since they're not paid – go off the boil. They'll give two years of their life, time and interest to the hobby of working for a charity or fund-raising organisation. Then they'll want to do something else. They get up to fever pitch of enthusiasm, and then it trails off.

So what you've got to do is squeeze 'em dry while you've got 'em, then go and find someone else!

Enthusiasm is the key to motivation

If I have anything going for me, it's my enthusiasm. I have got the ability to get monstrously enthusiastic about things. And that keeps me going.

It's important, therefore, to have an enthusiastic man or woman to head your organisation. I've found that if you are enthusiastic about things, that enthusiasm does tend to spill over to the people you're working with and who are listening to you. You motivate them by it.

You never know whom you'll meet...

One of the most rewarding things about charity work is the number of interesting – and surprising – people you'll find yourself coming into contact with.

I was once invited to the Ritz to meet the president of the Fitzroy Homes, who were after one of our 'NEW HORIZON' mini-buses. As I approached the hotel I was certain I knew what the lady would look like – stout, large-bosomed, with a raucous voice and a moustache.

Imagine my amazement when I met the Countess of Euston – a young swinger if ever there was one!

Fitzroy Homes got the bus and I got tremendous fun striding across the concourse at Euston Station – on my way to Birmingham, where the bus was to be given away – demanding of every railway official, 'Have you seen the Countess of Euston?'

Using people intelligently

One of the main functions of fund-raising efforts is to *motivate* your members, and get those who do nothing to do something. To be fair, it's very often because they haven't actually been asked.

And sometimes it isn't a lack of will, it's just that nobody's bothered to write to them or ring them up and say 'Would you like to consider doing this or that?' Many people don't like to push themselves forward, so make sure they don't have to!

Make the most of membership forms

The easiest way to find out about your members is on their membership forms. Don't simply ask their name and address, but what they like doing, and what they *can* do.

Find out, for example, their occupation (you never know when it can come in handy), their hobbies (someone who likes drawing and painting may be able to design your posters and handbills), what they enjoy doing (if they like socialising they'll be very useful at fund-raising events) etc.

Your membership forms should ensure you make the most of your members, and that they will get the maximum enjoyment out of working for your organisation.

But, of course, it's not always as straightforward as that. Our members have to fill in a form which asks 'What can you do to help our charity?' If you read these forms, it's sensational – they say everything, promise to do everything. But, as I say, often you get nothing from them.

What we do on the membership committee now is to take last year's crop and go through each one saying, 'What has he been doing for the past year?' And if the answer is 'very little' we get on to the chap who put him up for membership and we say, 'Mr Snodgrass has been asleep for the past year, would you like to wake him up and suggest he comes and joins us?'

But you've got to have something for that member to do.

Talent spotting

When appointing your committees and planning your events, you must always make sure you pick the right people for the right tasks.

Use your imagination. For example, the ideal person to run a bring-and-buy would be a local retailer, market stallholder or auctioneer – somebody used to selling to the public. If you haven't got one on your team, go out and recruit one!

(Conversely, if one of your members has a talent worth exploiting, think of ways to exploit it!)

On the other hand, though, it's no good asking a top businessman to run a bring-and-buy. He's unlikely to have the time or the expertise. Instead, write to him and say, 'Look, we're short of a sponsor for such and such. It costs £4,000. Would you like to do it?'

You've got to deal with each person according to his talents. His talent may be signing cheques.

School for thought

Schools are particularly good at fund-raising, and at providing manpower and labour when it comes to collecting things and money. Schoolchildren have often turned out at our cricket matches to sell raffle tickets and so on.

But, in the main, schools are so undercapitalised and have so many new projects of their own – fund-raising for school books and equipment, for example – that youngsters often have to hold charitable events for their own ends. And with homework taking up much of their time, it's unfair to *expect* them to pitch in with your events.

So if you do get support from local schools or clubs – or simply your own children – make the most of it:

Do...
encourage children to take part in sponsored walks, runs, swims, etc. Involving them in fund-raising when they're young will set a pattern for life.

Whatever the cause, they'll enjoy taking part in activities – and raising money into the bargain. The results will astound you, too – people find it difficult to resist children waving sponsorship forms!

But don't...
exploit children. Make sure their sponsored activities are safe, supervised, and well-organised. And that children are suitably dressed – wearing sturdy walking shoes, not plimsolls, for long distances, for example.

And never...
send children out alone, especially at night!

Put this in your pipe and smoke it!

It's the members of an organisation that make working for it both enjoyable and memorable.

I have particularly fond recollections of our former president, the late Eric Morecambe, who was an inveterate pipe smoker. At an event at Blenheim Palace, having been advised by his doctor to stop smoking, he suddenly pulled off the stem of his pipe, threw it away and handed me the bowl, saying, 'Have my pipe – you'll enjoy it.'

He had told me that it was a Dunhill, the *crème de la crème* of pipes, so I thanked him and, the next day, went off to Dunhill's in Jermyn Street to get it re-stemmed.

In fear and trepidation I entered the magnificent portals of the shop to enquire how much re-stemming would cost. Imagine my consternation when the smart shop assistant in white gloves quoted me £10 – I had never spent more than £5 on a pipe in my life!

Recovering from the shock, I tentatively enquired what kind of pipe it was, and the assistant looked at me disdainfully and said, 'Sir, it is our golden nugget'.

I then asked to see the range, which was elegantly displayed under a glass case, and my next question was the clincher: 'How much is your golden nugget?'

'Two hundred and fifty pounds, Sir,' was the reply.

So I rushed off to get my gold-bowled pipe re-stemmed – £10 was cheap at the price. And, to this day, every time I smoke that beautiful pipe I think of dear old Eric.

4 · The Set-up

Getting organised

The reason so many fund-raising organisations – and events – are not successful is because they're so boring. You've got to capture the public's imagination for your charity somehow or other. And it all boils down to the organiser, the person at the head of the organisation.

The importance of good management

Charity organisers, or directors, should be skilled people, paid a market salary. It should be an honourable profession. But it is still traditionally a kind of decent thing for ex-Service chaps, and I'm afraid that *has* to go – we've got to put some sharp, keen, highly paid, highly intelligent directors, men *and* women, in to run charities, and I reckon we could double the money collected overnight.

If you're starting a fund-raising organisation in a small way, of course, the whole thing will probably be voluntary. You can't afford to have a paid person running it. But, whatever the size of your organisation, you can't afford to ignore the importance of good management.

Remember that however well-meaning your volunteers, you must take a sensible, businesslike approach to staffing and delegation of the work otherwise you'll never succeed.

It's no good saying, 'Dear Mrs So-and-so is sweetly doing appeals this year. . . .' You don't want her – you want a hard-headed marketing person. Let her do the flowers or something instead.

The importance of targets

One of the main reasons that many fund-raising organisations fail is that they don't set themselves targets. You must always have an aim, or you'll simply limp along no particular route.

When we do the budgeting bit, we list all the events and we set targets against them. It was my idea to introduce targets and, to be quite frank, nobody wanted them — like most people, our members don't like targets.

They tell me, 'Let's see how it goes . . . let's have fun, and if we raise £500 that's great.' I reply, 'No, no, you're going for £5,000, buster!'

Everyone's got to know that, and got to report progress.

A target is the driving force, the motivator. It's terribly important.

It's not just for success in the short-term, either. It helps us plan for the future.

For instance, we look at our target and see if we've achieved it; the next year we look back at the figures and see that we set a target of £5,000 for this particular dinner but we only raised £4,000. So we carry on to the next year with the same target. Or, if we exceeded it, we'll load the target with another 20 per cent or something.

You need a target for each event, so the target figure becomes the total figure. Because we raised £700,000 in 1985 we went through all the events and budgeted for 1986, setting ourselves a target of £820,000, which we felt we could achieve easily. A far cry from the £18,000 we raised in 1972!

The importance of success

You definitely build on success, and if an event is not very successful the first year, I would always have a go the second time around. It's that much easier to organise — you'll know what went into it, which team of helpers to employ etc — and you might get it off the ground this time.

The importance of thinking big

However small your organisation, you've got to *think big* all the time. Here are three valuable tips:

1) Never underprice yourself. For example, if you've run raffles charging 10p a ticket, why not try 20p next time?

Or what about £1? You may think that the locals won't shell out £1 for a ticket, but if you offer the tickets at 20p each or 10 for £1, I bet you'll see plenty of £1 coins changing hands. People like to feel they're getting a good deal.

And you'll never know what the market will take till you try!

2) When you plan your fund-raising events, remember that it's far better to expend your skill and energy on running one or two big events than on several little ones which require just as much administrative effort. The rewards will be far greater – both in terms of cash raised and enthusiasm generated.

3) In all your fund-raising plans, you are out to capture the public's imagination; unless you achieve this, they will not be forthcoming with the purse. For instance, why not consider asking a well-known personality, who has already captured the public's imagination, to front your organisation?

Having said that, though, busy celebrities will need convincing that you deserve their time and attention, and will demand – quite rightly – an efficient organisation. If they appear at an event, they will expect to receive a proper brief and everything to go like clockwork.

They are professionals – like, no doubt, many of your members – and will not take kindly to an amateur approach, however small your fund-raising organisation. Remember, too, that they have their reputation to uphold – they have been associated with success, not failure.

But if you play your cards right, celebrities can open doors for you that you had never dreamed of.

Why you need a patron

Having a noticeable and notable name on your letterhead can only do you good. A patron gives your organisation credibility and can also be wheeled out on very special occasions to write or speak on behalf of the charity.

If you've had a good year, you might want your patron to write a congratulatory note you can send out to your members as a thank-you for past efforts and encouragement for future ones. Or you might want him or her to write a foreword in a brochure or to present a special prize or award.

You need someone instantly recognisable, in an exalted position, and with some permanence – such as an MP in a safe seat, a member of the local gentry or aristocracy, or a celebrity.

A royal patron, of course, can work wonders for your charity if you're lucky enough to get one. But remember: royalty are very busy people, with many equally important demands on their time, and you cannot therefore expect them to turn up to every event. (The same can be said for anyone else in public demand.)

Choose your requests wisely and take note that royal patrons plan their programmes six months in advance. So think ahead. And bear in mind that royal patronage is extended to literally hundreds of organisations – not just yours!

Get to know your patron's private secretary who, in my experience, can be extremely helpful. And always write to the private secretary – *never* write to royalty direct.

I brief Prince Philip on the progress of The Lord's Taverners about once a year, with particular emphasis on our financial progress and any new fund-raising events we have introduced. I also write to him frequently asking for messages to go in our various brochures and to sign letters on important subjects that are being sent to important people.

Three patron tips

1) Use your patron sparingly; no fund-raising organisation should expect its patron to make a personal appearance more than once a year, royal or otherwise. The more special or exclusive you make patrons, the greater the impact they will have when they do appear.

2) Make sure you invite your patron only to special events, not to any of your more mundane ones; and make sure that the occasion has good fund-raising potential so that you can capitalise on his or her presence.

3) If you want your patron to make a speech – and this particularly applies to royalty – make sure he or she is given a full brief with a draft speech.

Why you need committees

Everyone says the best committee is a committee of one, and this is true up to a point. But committee work is an inevitable part of charity administration, and you've got to have a structured committee to run the various elements of any fund-raising organisation.

To be a good committee member you have to be a good listener. You've got to be patient and expect lots of meetings where people will waffle on and on and drive you mad!

If, like me, you're the 'professional', it's tempting to think you know all the answers, but this must be supressed at all costs.

Appointing your committee

The chair

The chairman – or, of course, woman – of a fund-raising committee is absolutely vital. He must chair the committee as if chairing a board meeting. He's got to put a watch in front of him and say, 'Now, ladies and gentlemen, we'll finish all this in an hour and a half' and he's got to go through the agenda in a brisk, businesslike fashion. Remember that many volunteers may have little experience of committee work.

He should let everyone have his or her say – he shouldn't express his views until the others have expressed theirs, a mistake which chairmen often make: they're terribly tempted to say, 'We're going to talk about this, that and the other. My view is. . . .' Which actually kills the discussion.

He should say, 'We now have this subject on the agenda. Ladies and gentlemen, what are your views . . . can I have some comments? Mary . . .? George . . .?' Encourage them to speak, because many people are nervous of speaking publicly, and tend to sit back listening to the others.

A well-conducted meeting is vital because the only point of a meeting is to lay the action plan for fund-raising. It's not just a social gathering for a gossip. After listening to the discussion, the chairman must then summarise that action: he must say, 'I think, ladies and gentlemen, from your views, the concensus of opinion is. . . .' And if they agree with his views, that's how they're minuted: 'After discussion it was agreed that. . . .'

As well as conducting the orchestra – his fellow committee men and women – the chairman must remember that he's got a secretary there taking minutes. The minutes are supposed to be 'a true record of what went on' . . . well, a true record of everything

that went on would condemn the whole system!

It's terribly important that the secretary is looked after at meetings: the chairman needs to turn round and say, 'Don't write this down, this is all waffle.' But once a decision's been made and a conclusion drawn, he's got to say, 'Will you minute that.'

I always make a point of sitting the other side of the secretary so that if the chairman doesn't say anything I can give guidance on what should be written down. The secretary, of course, will have to type out the minutes in draft and send them to the chairman, because they're the chairman's minutes.

Once the minutes have been approved by the committee as being 'a true record' they have to be signed by the chairman.

The ideal chairman

1) He (or she) has to be firm, and able to think straight – he mustn't allow himself to deviate by red herrings and to be drawn away from the subject by someone who's a good speaker. Chairing a meeting is a great skill, almost an art form.

2) He's got to have a good personality because he's got to encourage people to talk, and get a decent concensus.

3) He's got to have self-restraint. He mustn't be too quick to make a judgment. And even if he knows where he wants the discussion to go he mustn't reveal it at the beginning of the game – he's got to let them all have their say and then gradually steer them and guide them down the route he wants them to take.

4) Above all, he should have a sense of humour. Some of the arguments get heated and some people get over-intense on a particular point of order.

Very often the best way to relieve the tension is to have a good giggle.

One final comment

The chairman is elected by the committee, so theoretically he or she is amongst friends. As chairman, therefore, you should aim for a working relationship based on friendship and trust.

The secretary

The voluntary secretary does exactly the same as the paid secretary. He or she's got to be good at taking notes quickly, ideally in shorthand. I've seen some secretaries operating with a tape recorder at meetings, but I think that's an absolute disaster because you've got so much filtering to do.

The secretary must be able to play an intelligent part in the subject under discussion and capable of eliminating the wheat from the chaff, which isn't always easy. Capable, too, of writing the standard reply letter.

My own secretary is my 'office wife'. In fact, she probably knows more about me than my wife does simply because of the amount of time I spend with her and the number of tasks we complete together. She knows my strengths, my weaknesses, my likes and dislikes. She knows what I'm like under strain, what I'm like at a party. And what a devil I can be when roused!

She runs the diary, keeps all my engagements going, sees that I'm decently presented to the outside world. She has to be very diplomatic and tactful; she must see that all correspondence is properly answered and that everything's put in front of me with a full brief. Some letters will even have a draft reply prepared.

We're very close because I depend on her totally. She is my right hand.

I believe you should always let your secretary know how valuable he or she is both to you and your organisation, because he or she can make or break you. It's important, too, to keep your secretary fully informed of everything that's going on so that he or she can act in your absence if necessary; and never forget to say where you'll be in those absences, so that your secretary can get hold of you without difficulty.

Never underestimate your secretary

Remember, when you have rattled off instructions to your secretary it is then that his or her work begins. The implementation of orders is sometimes more difficult than giving them.

The treasurer

The treasurer really is the custodian of the finances and should take his or her job very seriously. If a treasurer resigns, then I think the fund-raising group's in big trouble!

The treasurer is responsible to the Charity Commissioners and for getting the accounts up to trial balance for the annual audit. It's the treasurer's job to go and face the auditors and answer any qualifying statements they may make about the accounts. He or she also has to present the accounts at the Annual General Meeting; and then has to get them adopted and propose a vote of thanks for the auditors.

At The Lord's Taverners we have an assistant treasurer, who is our accounts person, because there's a hell of a lot of day-to-day bookkeeping involved.

Incidentally, the treasurer's statement, which is technical, should be typed out beforehand and an advance copy given to the secretary. Trying to get facts and figures down in shorthand at an annual general meeting can be difficult.

The power behind the throne . . .
The treasurer is a very powerful person because he or she should say yea or nay to expenditure, as well as seeing that debtors and creditors are handled properly. The treasurer doesn't, however, have to be an accountant or banker by profession – simply someone with an eye for detail and a way with facts and figures.

I personally feel that, in some organisations, treasurers tend to be too powerful.

To coin a phrase, I think treasurers should be on tap but not on top. In other words, they're there in an informative capacity, a supplier of facts and figures, but they shouldn't dictate to management the way the show's going to go.

They're custodians of the cash, yes, but not fund-raisers.

Additional committee members

The bigger your organisation, the more committee members you may want or need to appoint. Here are three of the most useful.

Publicity secretary
It's important to present your organisation to the great British public through the media. If you don't do that, nobody will bother with you at all because there's so much competition. You've got to

be in there shouting about your product as well as everybody else is.

The publicity person has to be a little bit of an extrovert and a personality, and capable of putting his or her views through strongly to get the attention of the media.

He or she's got to be fairly lively — in a nutshell, a salesperson par excellence.

Ideally, you need a PR person who knows everyone in Fleet Street — or can make himself or herself known to the people who matter on your local papers, at least! — with a flair for words and able to write and distribute a press release correctly (see page 63).

But a PR person is nothing without a good brief.

You could, of course, try and persuade a reputable public relations company to take you on for nothing. Many of the big companies are proud to hold a charity account as part of their service to the community.

But if you're a small local fund-raising group you'll be surprised at the amazing results you'll get simply by appointing an enthusiastic, imaginative and ambitious publicity secretary.

Membership secretary

You might want a membership secretary, a recruiting sergeant in a sense. Someone with a no-nonsense approach – and, again, a bit of imagination – who will go out and about getting supporters and helpers for your organisation, expanding your labour force. Because you've got to have helpers — you can't raise money with just a couple of people, however willing.

But your membership secretary also has to be of the charm school variety!

He or she has to go out spreading the gospel, saying, 'Come and join our cause, our charity is worthwhile, come and help us.' Doing the Billy Graham act locally, getting the people on board.

If your charity is holding a lunch, he or she should make sure that the chairman stands up and focuses attention on the fund-raising bit. He or she will also have the ultimate responsibility of standing up at the next monthly meeting and saying how many people have joined or resigned.

Above all, your membership secretary is the person in constant touch with the members of your society or association. And, believe me, members do need chatting up from time to time!

Time spent with a member is never wasted. They are the flesh and blood of the organisation. Angry members can do untold harm. Happy members can help you to prosper.

Social secretary

The social secretary is the person responsible for seeing that all your events run smoothly, attending to every detail from the table plan to the food. He or she can take a lot of weight off the chairman and secretary, as well as generating ideas as to what events should be held.

He or she's got to be a socialiser, happy mixing with people. A lively sort, with lots of contacts, who should never sit down at a lunch or dinner until everyone has found his or her seat.

(By the way, I had an occasion recently when an entire table of guests had been omitted from the seating plan of a dinner. So your social secretary should always remember to see that the banqueting manager has a spare table handy.)

10 things to remember about committees and committee meetings

1) The choice of representatives on a committee can make life easy or difficult for you. Try to achieve a good cross-section of personalities and skills.

2) See that your constitution legislates for members serving no longer than, say, three years before retiring compulsorily from the committee for a minimum period of three years. The introduction of new blood on to a committee is essential if it is not to become moribund. I know that using this method you will be losing some good people but, on balance, it is the most sensible way in which to manage your affairs.

3) Try to rationalise the number of committees you have. For example, we had a Public Relations Committee and a Publicity Committee, which we've now amalgamated under the heading of Marketing Committee.

4) Bear in mind that administrative time spent on committee work reduces the overall time given to fund-raising, to which you owe

your charity status. Think of all those agendas and minutes that have to be taken down in shorthand, typed and circulated!

5) Many of your charity problems will be resolved by discussion either before or after meetings. However, you cannot duck the issue of establishing committees for most areas of your work. With intelligent rationalisation and selection of their members, committees can serve a charity in a beneficial way.

6) If you have an idea that needs putting across, the legitimate use of lobbying is often a good way of overcoming these difficulties. I have often found it easier to propound my case beforehand to influential members of a committee, who will then fight my battles for me. Volunteers will more easily listen to the views of a fellow volunteer than to those of the professional.

7) If there are difficult subjects to be discussed, it is often wise to prepare a working paper beforehand to circulate to all members. Don't forget that your committee, although talented in their own sphere, often have to discuss matters which need a brief. You will have been dealing with the subject for weeks and your volunteer committees will need guidance to catch up with the argument.

8) Always prepare an agenda, which should be circulated to committee members before the meeting. A well-prepared agenda will enable a committee meeting to go with a swing; a badly-prepared agenda will make the meeting dull and sterile.

Agendas follow a set format in that there are at least four items which never change. These are:
a) apologies for absence
b) adoption/confirmation of the minutes of the last meeting
c) matters arising
d) any other business, usually followed by the date of the next meeting.

But it's the meat in the sandwich which should form the guts of the meeting.

I always make a point of writing to members of the committee calling for items for the agenda, because it is only if the committee members take an active part in the subject matter for the meeting that it will be a success.

Many points are forgotten at meetings, and the only way to see that they are not mislaid is to whack them down on the agenda, however trivial they may be. The chairman's job is then to conduct the committee through the agenda.

I personally am very hard on those who use 'any other business' as an excuse to pull a fast one on the committee; items for discussion should be included on the agenda, and 'any other business' used *only* for late, late entries.

9) Try to ensure that no member leaves a meeting without having agreed to do something positive. No committee member worth his salt should leave a meeting without a 'commitment' scribbled on the back of an envelope.

10) To drink or not to drink at the meeting? That's up to the chairman.

A little jungle juice can sometimes oil the wheels; too much can gum up the works.

By the way ...

Charities being labour-intensive, the Charities Aid Foundation (see Chapter 9) worked out that of the 200 top charities, every person employed raises £35,000 per annum out of the gross revenue raised by those 200 charities.

I'm very proud of the fact that, at the last count, my own staff each generated £140,000 – four times as much as the average!

5 · Administration

Office administration

However small or large your organisation, you must have a well-run office. If you don't, you'll find yourself wasting valuable time searching for documents and other paraphernalia when you should be out marketing your charity.

If you're a small group, you may find that one of your members has a spare room he or she is prepared to set aside as your office – ideally, your chairman or secretary, who will need to work there most often, dealing with correspondence.

You won't need much equipment – just a desk, filing cabinets and a typewriter to begin with – and you will probably be able to get these donated if you ask around. Companies are constantly refurbishing their offices and are often only too happy to pass on discarded, but perfectly functional, equipment.

But if you're a large group or registered charity and are setting up an office, you will need good people, adequate space and equipment.

All these running expenses add up to money or overheads, which should not exceed 20 per cent of your total revenue if you are to sell yourself to those who want to help you – eg sponsors.

The staff at HQ

Although every fund-raising group relies heavily on its voluntary brigade, its HQ staff will have the ultimate responsibility of running the show.

Besides the normal secretarial and administrative skills they must:

1) be both flexible and interchangeable. Most charities are too small to be departmentalised;

2) be good at dealing with members and voluntary workers who, as I have mentioned, sometimes have a natural antipathy towards the professionals – ie HQ staff;

3) be prepared to work long hours and on many occasions help to run events which do not finish before midnight. They'll need to be fully aware of this before accepting a job;

4) be capable of handling word processors and micro-computers. There is much charity information which is better off on software rather than on a card index; and, very often, policy decisions and strategy are dependent upon information supplied by the computer.

(By the way, with technology advancing so quickly these days, it's better to rent than buy equipment – all companies provide computer equipment, like TV sets, on either a rent or sale basis.)

Staff tips

1) It's essential to give all members of staff a job description. This does not mean that in a small charity an 'all hands to the pump' regime will not sometimes prevail; it does mean, however, that your staff will know exactly what their duties include, which is only fair and makes for the running of a smooth office.

They should all have a contract of employment; too often, this is overlooked.

2) Get the staff together at regular intervals to discuss the work of the organisation, keep them informed, and iron out any administrative problems.

Communication is the key to success.

3) Take an interest in your staff and their performance. Remember birthdays, and if you do have a sense of humour *use it!* Conversely, if you have a misfit on your staff, get rid of him or her immediately.

A lightweight in the team can lose the match.

4) Pay the going rate when it comes to salaries. Gone are the days when you could expect people to work for charity for virtually

nothing. The quality of your staff will depend largely upon paying them a market salary.

5) Jobs should be interchangeable in a small charity so that life is simple when someone goes on holiday. You don't want to have to employ 'temps', who are both costly and will not necessarily be as efficient and reliable as your own regular staff. But when employing staff through an agency, it's always worth stressing that you're a charitable organisation and asking for a reduction in the fee.

Filing tips

1) If you can't find a letter, the administration of your organisation will come to a grinding halt. So impress upon your filing person that he or she is doing the most important job in the office – which is true.

And make sure that filing is done first thing every morning. Don't let it pile up.

2) Devise a decent reference system, including a 'bring-up' file and a separate 'copy' file for all outgoing correspondence (on different-coloured paper, if possible).

3) Prepare pro-formas for repetitious items such as application forms for events. That way, you'll avoid wasting time.

Correspondence tips

1) Try to drop the time-wasting habit of drafting letters in longhand, and instead use dictation or, if you prefer, a tape recorder and audio-typing. I prefer dictating to my secretary, who plays the role of my correspondent; a good secretary, too, will often steer you towards the right choice of words.

2) Always 'top and tail' letters – that is, write in your own hand 'Dear Mr Smith' and 'Yours sincerely' – and attempt to personalise the address. If you don't know the name of your correspondent, find out!

3) Don't scribble all over your incoming mail. You may have to produce a copy letter sometime. If you want to give an instruction to your staff on a letter, use the removable coloured stickers now available from stationers.

Telephone tips

1) If, for one reason or another, the office is not manned all the time, it pays to get British Telecom to install an answering machine – useful, too, for outside working hours, when the office is closed. For the price of the rental, it would be foolish to miss a call from a potential sponsor or donor!

When you record your outgoing message, prepare carefully what you are going to say and don't make it too long-winded. But be polite and, if you like, mildly witty.

A friend of mine begins his message, 'Hello there. Why do all the nice people ring up when I am out?' Flattering, and gets them in the right mood to respond.

Alas, many callers still dislike speaking to an answer phone and will hang up after listening to the message, so a good friendly welcome which encourages them to speak is so important.

Change the script of the message from time to time, so that regular callers will be encouraged to listen. Remember, too, that the same voice can become boring so let your staff take it in turns to be the 'announcer'.

And don't forget to train your staff to get the message off the answer phone immediately they return to the office.

2) Make sure your staff remember to give you telephone messages – there is nothing more irritating and less professional than receiving a call from someone who says he has already rung you twice.

3) When making calls, train your staff to leave your name and telephone number if the person being called is unavailable. **It is a waste of charity money to call twice.**

4) Train your staff to get the actual person you wish to speak to on the line rather than leaving you 'holding on' to someone else's secretary.

Budget tips

1) Whenever I call upon a would-be sponsor, the first question he asks is 'How much in the pound goes to the customer?' The upper limit for expenses in my view should be 20 per cent. Evidence of tight control of overheads will impress modern-day sponsors, because they are hard-headed businessfolk who do not want to

give away their money – even pre-tax profits – to organisations who are profligate.

2) If expenses are getting out of control, look to the generation of more funds. Don't go around switching off all the lights and the heating without first thinking 'How can I generate more funds?'

The Lord's Taverners' cost ratio was out of balance one year, so we launched the Eric Morecambe Appeal for Youth, which netted an additional £100,000, getting us back to 82p in the £.

The interesting point here is that in subsequent years, we never lost that £100,000, although the appeal was only for one year.

One last word on the subject

While you stand on the bridge in command, never forget those sweating it out in the engine room.

Charity accounting

Charity accounting is most important. Under the 1960 Charities Act you will have to prepare annual accounts and this can only be done satisfactorily if your book-keeping has been accurate.

It is a good thing to discuss your accounting system with your auditor who will be able to give you the format in which he or she wants the accounts presented to trial balance.

Why not try and recruit an auditor on to your committee – just think of the money you could save!

Bills and invoices

It should go without saying that your accounts person must be diligent about getting money owing to your organisation into the coffers. He or she should send out invoices promptly and, conversely, take the maximum time for credit when paying your bills.

Never be embarrassed to invoice in advance, pointing out that you are a charitable organisation.

Unfortunately, many companies put charity bills at the bottom of their priority list for payment, whereas they should be at the top.

Worry them to death until you get the money!

Presentation of accounts

The presentation of your accounts is also important. Major donors will naturally want to see their name in print, so don't simply tuck them away under 'Donations'. You will have to provide the auditor with the names of the donors, together with the amounts, if they are to enjoy 'separate billing'.

The best way to decide who should be mentioned and who remains anonymous, in my view, is to spell out only the names of people who have donated over a certain amount, say £500.

Make sure you pay the right rates

The most a charity has to pay in rates is 50 per cent. The first 50 per cent is mandatory rate relief as laid down by the Government, provided the premises are being used wholly or substantially for charitable purposes.

In addition to mandatory rate relief, charities may apply to their local authority for discretionary rate relief on the remaining 50 per cent—though this is often restricted to charities whose fund-raising goes back into the locality. It is possible, therefore, in some cases, to avoid rates altogether.

Incidentally, in Northern Ireland, 100 per cent mandatory rate relief can be obtained — well done the Irish!

Certain non-registered charities are recognised by local authorities for discretionary rate relief; in these cases, the cost of discretionary relief is borne by local ratepayers.

All local authorities vary in their attitudes towards relief. So the first thing you should do is find out what the local government policy is for your area.

Be sure of insurance

A third party insurance policy is a must if you are staging any kind of public event. The Lord's Taverners have one for £2 million which covers liability for all our events, including twelve cricket matches.

Talking of cricket and insurance, some organisers of outdoor events take out a policy against rain — it's called a pluvius policy. But these policies are very expensive and you'll only get paid out if the rain is particularly heavy, though it only takes a drizzle to spoil an event. We prefer to gamble on a fine day!

Don't forget, too, that if your event is sponsored, the money will be in the kitty anyway, and sponsors are very honourable – they pay up, fair or foul.

Your bank account

Try to find a bank manager who will give you friendly terms. Play your cards right, for example, and you may get the bank to waive all bank charges. An unsecured overdraft can also come in extremely handy.

You'll have to agree who is to sign cheques before you fill in a bank mandate. If you want cheques issued in a hurry, the best thing is to have a two-tier system. For small amounts make it easy, but for larger amounts insist on a two-signature system, to include either the chairman or the treasurer.

Your treasurer – like ours – may insist upon signing all the cheques. Let him!

Petty cash

This is for small, incidental payments and should be kept by a responsible secretary, who should be the only person to hold the keys. He or she should always give and get receipts for cash transactions, and should make a note of the cost of items where receipts are unobtainable.

Petty cash can either be 'topped up' or you can run an 'imprest' system where the amount actually spent is paid back.

Never hold too much in petty cash, and have the amount reconciled once a week.

VAT

If your turnover is more than £18,000 you must be registered for VAT, and the VAT people give you a thorough inspection every three years. VAT is payable or reclaimable, depending on the circumstances.

You can reclaim the VAT on all expenses and invoices which include it. For example, hotel invoices, printing and stationery costs, prizes bought, T-shirts bearing your logo, etc.

On the other hand, you have to charge VAT on certain items. If, for example, you sell a dinner ticket for £30, £26.09 will go to your charity and 15 per cent, ie £3.91, will have to be handed back to Customs and Excise.

I've found this sometimes extremely difficult to get our volunteers to understand, because they think they have raised £30 and this often causes discussions at the end of the financial year.

Sponsors must also be charged VAT. On the whole, companies sponsoring events can reclaim the VAT.

Remember, if you don't charge VAT, you're still liable to pay it!

So when you're negotiating with a sponsor, always make sure to agree the grant as an *exclusive* amount, whereby VAT is added to the total paid to the charity.

Examples

a) Inclusive grant £10,000
   VAT £1,300
   Net available to charity £8,700
   Gross amount paid
   by donor **£10,000**

b) Exclusive grant £10,000
   VAT in addition £1,500
   Net available to charity £10,000
   Gross amount paid
   by donor **£11,500**

As you can see, this will benefit your organisation as it will be able to offset any input tax paid on goods and services it purchases in the process of spending the grant.

In most cases, donors will not mind whether VAT is added or not; so it is encumbent upon you to agree a VAT-exclusive figure.

Donations, however, are not subject to VAT – they're called 'zero-rated' – and certain areas are partially exempt, which involves using a complicated formula to assess the tax. The VAT people will be able to give you more details and advice here.

Your local VAT inspector will come along to your office to do a VAT audit. This can be hair-raising but, on the whole, if you are honest the VAT people can be very helpful.

To sum up

1) You must fill in your VAT return at the end of each quarter, which involves 'inputs' and 'outputs'. Inputs are monies you are claiming back and outputs are monies you have to pay Customs and Excise. When you balance up you'll see whether you need to pay the difference to Customs and Excise, or they to you.

2) If your VAT return is not sent within the time limit, Customs and Excise can exercise their right to charge interest on the money owed, and they are now becoming stricter. In our case, this means that we must chase our regions for information on sale of tickets and sponsorship, because if we don't declare it in time we may be liable for interest.

3) It's a good idea to get the local VAT officer on your side. Invite him (or her) along to meet you. I'm certain you'll find him very helpful.

4) If your turnover's within the threshold, you've got no problem. But if you exceed the threshold the answer really is to get as much of your income donated or covenanted as you can. (See Chapter 9.)

USEFUL ADDRESSES: In all matters of accounting I'd strongly recommend you consult an accountant. If you don't know one personally, you could consult one of the major accounting bodies which include the following:

a) The Institute of Chartered Accountants in England and Wales, PO Box 433, Moorgate Place, London EC2P 2BJ;

b) The Institute of Chartered Accountants of Scotland, 27 Queen Street, Edinburgh EH2 1LE;

c) The Institute of Chartered Accountants of Northern Ireland, 11 Donegall Square South, Belfast BT1 5JE;

d) The Association of Certified Accountants, 29 Lincoln's Inn Fields, London WC2A 3EE;

For advice on all aspects of VAT registration, contact the Hon VAT Advisor, National Council for Voluntary Organisations, 26 Bedford Square, London WC1B 3HU.

Regional development

As your organisation grows, you may well consider having branches throughout the country. But, as I've discovered, central control and co-ordination become more important — yet more difficult — as the number of branches increases.

Branch members must uphold charity law and stick to the rules of your organisation; too many people are only too pleased to 'buck the system' if they can get away with it.

It is essential, therefore, to keep everyone in the picture with a set of guidelines and clearly defined parameters within which they can operate. And you must establish a good working relationship between your branches and headquarters.

Guidelines

Again, from experience, these must include precise rules on accounting procedures — the amount of VAT money The Lord's Taverners have failed to recover in the past from our regions, due to lack of understanding, is appalling.

If you have a central investment policy — and you *should* have one — it is essential that net profits from regional fund-raising events should be forwarded to HQ without delay, together with an income and expenditure statement. (See Chapter 9 for investment advice.)

Believe me, this will often be resented by your fund-raisers out in the sticks, but money makes money.

There is no point having large sums sitting in current or deposit accounts when they should be helping your central investment programme. Literally thousands of pounds from investment can be lost by ignoring this point.

And all regional accounts should be audited at the end of your financial year.

Keeping in touch

Frequent visits to your regions, though time-consuming, are very important. Letters can be misunderstood, and an eyeball-to-eyeball meeting is always preferable to sending a set of rules through the post. This all adds up to good and sensible management.

In a word, don't get into correspondence battles with your

different areas – go and see them.

A case for participation

Regional participation is crucial to your overall fund-raising campaign. Regional members should be free to exploit innovative ideas and encouraged to disburse locally any funds raised locally. This is not only good for the morale, but adds to the influence and authority of regions.

And a final word on the subject

Give plenty of time and thought to regional expansion. If your charity is well spread geographically throughout the country, you could become a household name.

6 · Advertising and Marketing

The hard sell

In order to 'sell' your organisation to the public at large, you have to market it as you would any other product. And successful marketing involves a mixture of advertising, publicity and public relations.

Let us take them one by one, although they are invariably interrelated.

Advertising

Advertising is very expensive and in many cases it's hard to tell whether it is paying off. If you decide to advertise your organisation, therefore, make sure you do it well!

There are two types of advertising:

1) *General advertising*

This is to keep your organisation in the public eye and needs to be done professionally. It's really only major charities who can afford this kind of advertising since to get any effect a charity must appear *regularly* in the national media, with an advertising campaign that can cost literally hundreds of thousands of pounds.

Remember, if you are thinking about a national advertising campaign, you will need to appoint a good advertising agency to handle it, and to make sure your advertisements appear in the appropriate media.

For press advertisements, you *must* aim for a design and copy which strikes directly at the conscience. A good example is

Mencap's national campaign headed 'What have you given to Mencap today?' Under the caption is a drawing of an unhappy looking child, and the effect is both emotive and immediate.

2) *Advertising for a specific event*

If you want people to turn up to your event, it's a good idea to get it advertised in the newspaper local to where the event is being held.

Many newspapers have a 'forthcoming events' section, which can save you having to pay for placing an advertisement. But even if you *are* taking an advertisement, don't forget to send a press release to the relevant editor (see page 63) as well; editorial coverage will not only serve as a form of free advertising but will also show the public that you're newsworthy and reputable.

There's also nothing to stop you promising to buy an advertisement on the condition that you get some free editorial with it; lots of advertisers do, and get away with it. It's certainly worth a try!

You should also try to get your event mentioned on radio (see page 65) and TV, especially if any big names will be there. A few years ago, for example, before our annual Henry Cooper boxing evening, I arranged for Henry and I to go on the Brian Matthews Show on Radio 2 to talk about the event. We were attempting to get 800 bottoms on seats and we succeeded.

On another occasion, when we were staging the Harry Secombe Golf Classic, we got Harry to pre-record a tape inviting the public to support the golf day. This went out on Capital Radio at regular intervals and we had a record crowd.

Brochures

Another very effective means of advertising is your organisation's brochure – and every reasonable sized charity should have one. Again, this requires a professional production if you're to look pukka and well-organised.

Try to get the brochure paid for by donation. This shouldn't be difficult if you go about it with determination: any sensible business person should see the advantages to his or her company of sponsoring a charity brochure – and, if not, point them out. Impress upon them that they're getting a great deal of advertising for their money (their company's name will be printed on every brochure and mentioned whenever possible: for example, in press releases) and that being associated with such a generous gesture can only do them good.

From your point of view, stating on your brochure: 'This brochure has been sponsored by . . .' will also handle any complaints about lavish spending!

If you're a large organisation, you may employ an advertising agency to help you with your brochure, particularly when there is artwork (ie illustrations and design features) involved.

An organisation with a smaller budget should look around for a good small agency or local studio to produce their brochure at a price they can afford.

Whatever the size of the agency, its copywriters can only write good copy if you provide them with sufficient information.

A brochure should include:

1) The name of your organisation and a snappy headline or slogan

2) Good photographs and drawings

3) Interesting text

4) A patron's endorsement

5) Details on how to give

6) A reply coupon for (5)

Our brochure is sent to everyone who inquires about our charity. It is also included in many of our mail-shots. You never know what interest it will generate.

Leaflets and letters

The same amount of preparatory work has to go into a leaflet or on a straightforward appeal letter. Remember that this leaflet will need updating from time to time.

The annual report

Your annual report and accounts is also a form of advertising and should be well presented but not so glossy that you solicit complaints about big spending. Some charities, in my opinion, spend too much money on their annual report and accounts. If you can get this publication sponsored, all to the good.

Programmes

Another form of advertising is to produce a programme to tie in with a fund-raising event. The most important factor is to assess advertising revenue, which will dictate the format and number of pages in your programme.

The revenue from advertising in your programme should be your biggest money-spinner.

Programme production

The shape and size

When planning your programme, the first thing to decide on is its format.

Printers' machinery is designed to cope with certain paper sizes prefixed by the letter A, and the two most common sizes for programmes are:

A4   11¾in x 8¼in, or 297mm x 210mm
A5   8¼in x 5⅜in, or 210mm x 148mm (ie, half the size of A4)

The size depends on your individual needs – what must be included, how much money you have to spend, and how you want the programme to look.

Once you have decided on the size, the next consideration is the number of pages. The pages in your programme will be printed in sections of four pages, so it will be a 4, 8, 12, 16, 20-page programme or more.

Let us assume that you decide on a 16-page programme. It will be made up as follows:

Front cover, inside front cover, back cover, inside back cover	4 pages
Editorial and advertising pages	12 pages
	16 total

Your format is now established so you're in a position to get a print quote, which will be based on the quantity of programmes required and the number of colours to be used in the printing. The cheapest colour combination is black on white; extra colours, though attractive, are costly.

Advertising revenue

Once you've got your print quote, you can then set your advertising rate, based on the number of spaces to be sold in relation to editorial and photographs.

Let us assume that your 16-page programme is made up as follows:

Front cover – charity logo and photograph.

Inside front cover – advertisers. (Higher than standard rate as this is a premium position.)

Pages 1 to 12 – four pages of editorials plus programme of events. Advertisers take up the remaining eight pages.

Inside back cover – advertisers. (Again, higher rate, premium position.)

Back cover – advertisers. (Higher rate, premium position.)

Out of the 16 pages available there are 11 to be sold. You can now set your rate per page for advertisers, and produce what is called a rate card.

Advertisement sizes

I have found from previous charity programmes that it is better to offer only half pages or full pages. This is because the smaller quarter pages are usually supplied by local businesses and, because of the work involved, generally cost more to put together than the cost of the space.

Cutting costs

The presentation of artwork by advertisers is all-important. Ill-prepared artwork (usually in a number of different elements) costs you more to prepare than what is known as 'camera-ready artwork' from which the printer can make his printing plates directly, without any extra work.

The more complete the artwork supplied by advertisers, the less extra costs are involved in your final invoice. Some advertisers will supply text only and will want the printer to typeset their advert (usually in the form of a short congratulation). Both these forms of advertisements are best for ease of programme make-up.

Programme administration

Apart from your committee and 'friends' selling space, it is essential to have one member of your committee responsible for:

1) liaising with advertisers or their agencies

2) receiving all artwork

3) liaising with printer

4) invoicing advertisers

5) writing editorial and organising photographs

Some advertising agencies will expect a 10 or 15 per cent commission for placing a client's advertisement. Inform them that it is a charity programme, so no agency commission is given.

Timing

Start planning your programme in plenty of time. Remember that the person you appoint to handle it – as well as many of your advertisers – may well have little experience of programme production, so do make sure you build in plenty of extra margins.

For a programme of 16–24 pages you should allow the printer three weeks to make up and print your programmes once he has received all the artwork, editorials and photographs.

It is not impossible to do the job faster, but it *is* unreasonable. Remember that if the printer is doing the job at cost price or below, you can't expect him to drop all his other commitments to rush your printing through.

The results

For a small programme, say A5, one colour, 24 pages, it is possible to achieve the following results:

Advertising revenue	£3,250
Printing, typesetting and make-up	£500
Profit	£2,750

You will see from the above example that it pays dividends to have a programme for an event – provided, of course, that your space-sellers do their stuff.

For example, at The Lord's Taverners' annual ball we produce a 100-page programme and raise £30,000 from advertising out of a total revenue of £50,000 for the event.

Publicity and PR

These are the life-blood of your organisation. Unless people know of your existence, they cannot help!

Publicity ranges from putting details of your fund-raising group on the noticeboard in your local library, to sending information to the press.

The press are on your side

One of the things you must remember is that if you're organising an event for a local charity or group, it's *not* national news. So you've got to write that out of your mind and concentrate on the local press. Unless, of course, there's a scandal, or a murder, or something!

The local press is always looking for copy, and if you offer to tell them about your fund-raising effort their response is likely to be, 'I'd like to hear what this person's got to say'. So I don't think it's very difficult to get them to turn up at your event – unless, unfortunately, there's some sort of crisis on that day in which they're all involved.

The press release
1) The right approach

A few days before your event, you should send a press release – ie a page of details about the event – to all your local newspapers. If you need help with their names and addresses, they'll all be listed in a publication called *Brad*, which you should be able to find at your local library.

Your press release should be as short as possible – no longer than one page of text, in double spacing and with wide margins – and it should be on notepaper that says 'Press Release' right across the top, and 'Further information from . . .' right across the bottom.

If you can afford it, it's better to have printed paper; it's more professional. Alternatively, you could buy a decorative rubber stamp with an ink pad, which will work out cheaper. (You can always make use of the ink pad in the future – with stamps for particular projects, for example.)

It's very important that the press release ties everything up: time, date, place. And that you give the press release a decent heading, which should encompass all that:

> There will be a dinner at Such-and-such Hotel
> at 7.30pm for 8pm on 27th March . . .
> Dress, black tie

That way, the journalist can see at a glance what the story's about before he or she starts to read all the facts.

2) The right angle

The other thing a reporter wants from a press release is an 'angle', and, unfortunately, that is always the most difficult thing. Ronnie Barker breaking his leg and being rushed to the local hospital is the kind of thing that makes headlines after the event, but no-one will give a toss about the fête he was attending; and, besides, the main purpose of the press release is to promote the event *in advance*.

So when you're writing your press release you've got to think of a way to personalise the event, to attract not only the attention of the editor but also the attention of the public.

It shouldn't be too difficult – in fact, the chances are that there's a strong story behind why you're raising money. Perhaps the cash will be used to send a child abroad for a life-saving operation, for example.

The press love a human interest story, so if you've got one, exploit it!

If you don't have a real story to tell, just dream one up! Home in on the one well-known personality and say something about him or her, backed up with a good quote from the celebrity if you can.

For example, if you were publicising a golf event, you might say something like, 'Terry Wogan's taken up golf! For the first time, you can see Terry playing. . . . He tells me he's been practising every day. . . . He's only been playing. . . .'

3) The right person

When you send out a press release it must always be accompanied by a personalised covering letter to the editor, or the sports editor – or whoever is responsible for the subject you're writing about. It's not difficult to get the name you want – just ring up and ask who deals with sport/events/whatever.

The covering letter is particularly important because every day an editor or sports editor gets a stack of press releases on his or her desk. You've somehow got to make sure yours doesn't end up in the wastepaper basket, and that one of the newspaper's minions is sent to cover your event.

The associate editor of the *Sunday Express*, Ken Lawrence, who's a good friend of mine and serves on The Lord's Taverners' council, warned me that without a personalised letter a press release on mundane matters will go straight into the dustbin.

However, if it says, 'Dear Ken, I do hope the Sunday Express will be able to use the enclosed . . . I've written all the details out for you. . . . Hope you can use it. . . . Yours . . .' it'll stop him chucking it away.

If there's a personal letter with your press release, the recipient will be much more likely to deal with it.

Things you might like to know about the press . . .

1) They tend to be rather disorganised
They're not in this world for politeness and exchange of letters and so on. Don't be surprised if they turn up without having acknowledged your invitation.

2) They like short cuts
They love handouts – they don't want to sit down with a shorthand pad. So if you can say, 'There you are, that's what I'm going to talk about . . . all the facts are there, buster, so all you need to do is listen to me', you can't lose!

3) They should be looked after
Give journalists a few gin and tonics and they're on your side. But don't expect them to spend any money themselves.

The press are, however, friendly people so take time to chat to them; don't treat them like complete peasants. In fairness, too, they're generally sympathetic to charitable causes.

Broadcasting your appeal
Charities don't make enough use of local radio. Bear in mind that

these poor devils have to fill up programmes twenty-four hours a day, so if you've got a good story to offer them they may well be happy to broadcast it.

Local stations are everywhere. There are something like thirty-five BBC radio stations in the country and forty-eight independent radio stations. And they are there to serve and report on local events; that's part of their franchise from the Independent Broadcasting Authority.

Do your homework: switch on and listen to the sort of thing they talk about. Then just ring up, ask for the station manager, and tell him or her what you have to offer.

For a local station, a well-known star opening your fête is a big event. And if there's nothing exciting happening at your 'do' you've just got to colour the pill to make it look like a Smartie.

You've got to say it's the BIGGEST and GREATEST . . . you've got to *sell*. Charity work is *selling*.

When a lady fell for Harry Secombe

Intelligent press releases, stories with an angle, are the type of things the media will latch on to. They are not terribly interested in statistics, they like happenings.

I remember Harry Secombe one day felling a lady with his drive off the first tee at Effingham Golf Club. She was struck on the temple by Harry's golf ball and went down like a sack of spuds. Harry, naturally, was very upset and concerned for the dear lady – who, I am happy to say, speedily recovered.

The point I am making, though, is that the Harry Secombe Golf Classic hit the national press that day – but only because of the incident I have described.

Other ways of getting your name into public consciousness

To make the name of your organisation a household word you must use your creativity. Dream up new schemes that will capture the public's imagination and have them reaching for their purses whenever they see your collecting boxes.

Here are a couple of ideas that will bring in money and promote your name at the same time. While they're primarily aimed at large charities, they should start you thinking of smaller schemes you might consider.

1) Endorsements

If you're a nationally-known organisation you could offer your charity's name to endorse products and ask for a fee for everything that's produced with your name on it. For example, if you're a sports-oriented charity, you could offer your logo to a sports goods manufacturer. But do make sure that the product doesn't reflect badly on your charity.

2) Books

You could approach publishers to see if your charity's name could be associated with anything they're producing. For example, we're associated with a series of books on cricket, and all the books carry our name in their title: *The Lord's Taverners Cricket Clinic*, etc.

As well as your charity's name appearing on bookshelves throughout the country, you should get royalties on sales, which can be very high if the book's a success.

If the book is written by a member of your organisation, or someone who has a particular interest in your cause, you might persuade them to donate their royalties, or a percentage of them, to your charity. Michael Caine, for example, has recently donated all the proceeds from the sale of his book to the National Playing Fields Association.

Even if you can't get your charity's name actually on a book, you could try encouraging a publishing company to donate a small percentage of the sales of one of their books to your charity – say, a few pence a copy. If the book is associated with your cause it may be easier to convince them, but there's really nothing to stop you picking any current best-seller! It needn't cost the publishers a fortune, and it's good publicity both for you and for them. If the author lives in your area, it makes an even better story.

The worst that can happen is that the publishers refuse. But, as they say, nothing ventured, nothing gained.

Words of wisdom

Producing books for The Lord's Taverners has given me great pleasure – not least our best-seller, 'The Fifty Greatest Cricketers'.

The idea came to me when a commercial artist friend of mine came to my office one day with a magnificent tome under his arm which he had just bought in New York. It was an illustrated book of famous baseball players: on one side was an artist's impression of the player and on the other an editorial about the player and his achievements. I asked whether he could get a team of artists together so that we could do the same for cricket, and he agreed to try.

The next problem was to agree a format – how many cricketers, who should be included, etc? I needed, therefore, an authoritative view and asked Trevor Bailey (Essex and England) if he would form a small selection committee. He agreed, bless him, and Richie Benaud, Jim Laker and Colin Cowdrey formed the august committee.

They held a dinner one evening in Birmingham after one of the Edgbaston Test matches, and I was privileged to be a fly on the wall. Mercifully, I had the wit to ask the publishers if they would pick up the tab for the dinner, for it went on into the early hours and became very expensive!

We decided upon fifty post-war cricketers. The first thirty were reached with complete unanimity: Bradman, Compton, May etc. Then the cut and thrust bargaining began, with Australian Richie Benaud fighting his corner like a tiger.

After the selection had been made each artist – there were four – was given a proportion of them; we arranged to have the editorial written by a talented cricket aficionado, and the end product was magnificent.

The book was launched in 1983 to much acclaim, and raised over £20,000 for our charity. It is still selling.

A job for the professionals?

There are a number of professional fund-raisers who will, for a fee or a percentage of the proceeds, raise money for your cause. Where it might prove difficult to get together a group of enthusiastic local people to do the job, this could well be a solution.

Professional fund-raisers do not have to be registered but the better ones are members of the Institute of Fund Raising Managers (see Appendix), who have a strict code of conduct.

Did you know that Jeffrey Archer was a professional fund-raiser at an early stage in his career?

On the whole, professional fund-raisers are good people and do a good job of work, but I would advise you to tread warily:

1) Don't appoint a fund-raiser until you've checked on his or her track record. Ask about previous clients, and get in touch with them to confirm that he or she did a good job.
2) Do make sure that the contract you sign with a fund-raiser has clearly defined break clauses, fee levels and expenses. Personally, I should always recommend going for a fee rather than allowing the fund-raiser to take a percentage; if he or she raises a huge sum of money, the less you have to give away, the better!

When professional help can be appealing . . .

It should also be said that registered charities often employ professional assistance in appeals. If I may quote an example of fees, professional fund-raisers Craigmyle & Co have this to say:

> Fund-raising on a significant scale must inevitably involve costs. The real test of whether the fee and expenses are cost-effective is the ratio of cost to the amount raised.
>
> Thus, an appeal costing £10,000 which raised only £25,000 would be regarded as too expensive, whereas an appeal costing £30,000 which raised over £300,000 could be regarded as good value for money.
>
> Over the years our fees have averaged about 4.5% of the sums raised and administrative costs another 4%. We do not offer a service unless we consider the cost will be justified by the results.

7 · The Main Events

The rules of the game

Competition is healthy

Make no mistake about it, charity work is a very competitive business. The size of the charity cake is limited, and there are many people after it.

There's also a limit to the amount that individuals are prepared to give, when they are constantly faced with appeals for charitable causes. And as more and more emphasis is being placed on self-help in the community — with many people now having to become involved in raising money for their own family's health and education — it's not surprising that the public is beginning to be more selective about its donations.

Having said this, the overwhelming success of appeals such as Live Aid, the BBC's annual Children In Need appeal, and Capital Radio's Help A London Child, has proved that the more that charities are seen to be doing good, the more charity-aware the market will be.

For as well as bringing in record amounts of cash for very worthwhile causes (and it's worth bearing in mind that every year the amount of money raised increases dramatically as individual fund-raising groups compete to collect the most and hit new targets), these well publicised events have also stimulated fund-raising right across the board — triggering off an incredible number of creative fund-raising ideas and incentives, and attracting participants and donors from every age group and walk of life.

But remember: to be successful a charity must be — and be seen to be — more dynamic, emotive and professional than its competitors.

Never look over your shoulder

Comparison between different charities' fund-raising methods are a waste of time. You are never comparing like with like.

If I compared The Lord's Taverners' fund-raising efforts with the Variety Club, for example, I should be making a grave error of judgment. We are essentially both a club and a charity, with a number of non-fund-raising club events; the Variety Club is high-pressure fund-raising all the way. And while I admire them enormously, it would be foolish to emulate them since their members include all the top people in the world of entertainment. A powerful lobby indeed.

Have confidence in your own programme

Remember that would-be benefactors will be quick to spot your deficiencies, so hurry up and get your act together.

Don't worry if you clash with another event

You don't intentionally set yourself to clash with another event, but if you accidentally do, just go flat out to get a full turnout for your occasion.

It's happened to us, and invariably we've not been affected by it – it must mean that there are always plenty of supporters around! It's also, of course, widening market awareness.

A prime example of this phenomenon is the fast-food business. When McDonald's hamburgers came to this country, Kentucky Fried Chicken got terribly worried that it might go out of business; in fact the opposite happened. The fast-food business became even more popular, and Kentucky Fried Chicken had an enormous increase in custom.

The more events the merrier, it seems – just as long as they're good.

Don't forget, though ...

You can't charge money at the gate on a Sunday. Instead, you have to have 'admission by programme', which means you must sell all the tickets in advance.

The big event

There's nothing like a big 'do' to bring your cause to the attention of the public, motivate your members, and raise a decent amount of cash. And one of the best crowd-pullers is a celebrity.

So before we get down to the nitty-gritty of organising a fund-raising event, here are some tips on how to get celebrities – and what to do with them once you've got them.

Why you need a celebrity

While it's not absolutely essential to have a celebrity at your event – and, of course, it's not always possible to get one – there's no denying the advantages. A well-known personality will attract a crowd, and a crowd will bring in the money.

In fact, the chance to see a famous person in the flesh is often the real reason many people will turn up; they're not *really* interested in buying secondhand books or whatever.

It doesn't matter who you choose, since the objective is simply to draw in a crowd; but, of course, from a publicity point of view it's particularly helpful if you can get someone who's known for his or her association with whatever your cause is.

How you get them

There is no set format for getting hold of a celebrity. It may also prove difficult because every summer there must be thousands of fêtes up and down the country, all of whom are trying to get hold of a star name. In addition, someone famous is only going to come and open your fête if he or she believes in your charity.

The best approach, I reckon, is by personal contact. Ask around to see who knows someone famous. For example, when we were to present a mini-bus at Chailey Heritage recently, we discovered that the Governor of Chailey Heritage was a personal friend of Simon Williams, who turned up – to the crowd's delight – with his old mate Nigel Havers. So we got two well-known faces for the price of one.

You could try tackling one of the stars who's appearing at your local theatre. I would probably rush round to the stage door and say, 'Hello, you won't know me. . . . My name's. . . . I'm running this great event on. . . . Could you come along to it – we'll pay your expenses? We're trying to raise money for the local hospital (or whatever) for x, y, z. . . . I do hope you can help us.'

Or if Willie Rushton, or whoever, happens to use the pub down the road, tackle him there. Celebrities generally understand unconventional approaches and unconventional people, and on the whole they're hopeless correspondents – they're unlikely to answer a letter (Willie Rushton, in fact, claims he chucks all his mail in the wastepaper bin!).

Showbiz personalities may also be contacted via the TV or radio station on which they appear; if a celebrity's written a book you could contact him or her via the publisher; if it's a journalist or someone who contributes to a newspaper, write to him or her via the newspaper or magazine.

If all else fails, you could also try *Spotlight* – a professional index of all actors and actresses, which you may find in your local library. It lists the names and addresses of their agents, who may be able to help.

Or: *Artistes and Their Agents*, published annually by J. Offord Publications, 12 The Avenue, Eastbourne, East Sussex BN21 3YA. At the time of writing this costs £7.95 (plus £1.25 p & p). And: *Who's Who on Television*, published by ITV Books and Michael Joseph, available from most bookshops, price £5.95.

When to book them
One thing you'll never be able to do is book a celebrity far in advance. A six-month booking – forget it! No actor will commit himself six months ahead. You're just as likely to get him (or her) the night before if you ring and he happens to be free the next day. If there's time, it's a good idea to write and confirm that he's going to appear.

Remember, though, that if work comes along you've got to expect your little charity 'do' to go out of the window. That's something you've got to accept. If, however, you book a celebrity on a professional basis – ie for a fee – then he'll be bound to turn up.

Why they might say yes
I'm full of praise for celebrities and the way in which many of them devote so much time to charities. But I have a sneaky feeling it's a two-way thing. I mean, they can't all be plaster saints and we're all the sinners!

I think it's good for their public image. If we have a cricket match, for example, it's no bad thing for the commentator to be continuously shouting a lesser known actor's name over the microphone to an audience of five thousand people. Celebrities sit in an autograph tent and sign programmes and say 'Hello darling, what's your name? etc,' and everyone goes away with a warm feeling, saying what a nice person the star is. So that must be good for their business.

What to do with them once you've got them

Once you get a celebrity to your event, it's terribly important to make sure he or she's looked after. You don't want your star to go away and say 'Never again!'

I took our president, Terry Wogan, to a dinner dance in Jersey, where we were both seated at the top table. At the end of the dinner, Terry and I looked around and the whole of the top table – the chairman etc – had all gone off somewhere with their mates.

I moved my chair next to Terry's and he said, 'Blow this for a lark, Tony, who's looking after us?' The next thing, he was descended upon by Jersey's blue-rinse brigade and I found myself acting as a sort of minder. Terry danced with them bravely for an hour or so, then, when the band finished, we scarpered. We went back to our hotel, and Terry went back to his room to relax.

The organisers of this event had committed the cardinal sin: they had ignored their guest of honour, left him unprotected and therefore at the mercy of the public. They didn't look after him, which is unforgivable.

(The next day, they even had the nerve to say, 'What happened to the President and Director? – I gather you both pushed off'!)

So the moral of the story is, don't let your celebrity out of your sight all evening if you're the chairman or organiser of the event. And find out what his (or her) mood is – whether he wants to go to the loo, wants to sit down, wants to dance.

Treat your celebrity like royalty, whoever he or she is.

Things to remember . . .

1) Your celebrity is probably as nervous as you

However well known he or she is, your star is bound to be very nervous. He's out of his natural habitat; he's not on stage with a big band and his name in lights and the audience told to applaud . . . He's Terry Wogan, or whoever, on his tod.

Some celebrities are very shy: Pete Murray's mum, for instance, sent him to RADA on their doctor's advice because he was such a shy, retiring boy – and many find it difficult to make speeches etc. So assume your celebrity is nervous and apprehensive, and make him feel at home, feel loved, wanted.

Find someone who's good at talking to follow your star around all the time. Never just give him a drink and then push off; he's most likely to just stand there and think 'What am I going to do now?'

2) Never expect them to make an off-the-cuff speech

Celebrities are always called upon to speak, but never expect them to come up with something off-the-cuff. Warn them you'd like them to say a few words at the event, and if possible send them something they can learn by heart if they wish, particularly if you want them to talk about the charity.

From my experience, the people who can't put the charity cause across seriously are the stars. The late Eric Morecambe, who was our president for three years, was a tireless worker for The Lord's Taverners but incapable of making a speech about the charity. He was so naturally funny that it was difficult sometimes to get back to the charity gospel. Besides, the public always expected Eric to make them laugh.

When we were launching the Eric Morecambe Appeal, Edward Heath leaned across to me and asked, 'Would you like me to say a few words?' I said 'Yes, please' and he got up and made a party political broadcast – he talked about the falling-down cities, the youth of Britain needing looking after, and he had the press eating out of his hand. They were writing it all down.

And as he came back he said quietly, 'I thought Eric needed a little help.'

Perhaps there's something to be said for choosing a politician as your celebrity.

3) Make sure your charity gets a mention

Don't forget to structure your presentation and butt in briefly to mention your charity and thank the celebrities and the fund-raisers for making the day possible etc before saying, 'Nanette Newman (or whoever) will now hand over the keys/cheque/whatever'.

4) Avoid 'frivolous billing'

One of the things that annoys celebrities more than anything else

– and I'm afraid it happens all the time – is what I would call 'frivolous billing'. People will put a poster up saying 'Terry Wogan is coming to this event . . .' and that brings the customers in.

But he probably wasn't even asked – or if he was, they've made an assumption that wasn't even there. He probably said, 'I don't know, it's most unlikely but I'll let you know.' So they put in small print: 'We have invited TERRY WOGAN'.

It's happened to us: we lost all support from John Alderton after an event at Blenheim. Someone put him in the team and he never said he would play.

On another occasion we announced that Terry Wogan would be playing in our Arundel cricket match. Apparently, Terry had said nothing of the kind, and through his Radio Two programme put out a complete denial. He also lambasted me by name.

I have every sympathy with this fierce reaction. Celebrities are extremely sensitive when it comes to letting down the public. The public, after all, are their bread and butter.

Moral: Nothing annoys anyone with a reputation more than being billed and not turning up – it's bad for their image.

5) Remember to say 'thank you'
Whenever a celebrity turns up, do write afterwards to say 'thank you so much, we do appreciate your help. . . .' You never know, you may need his or her support again in the future.

The obvious schemes

There are two main fund-raising events which every organisation may want to hold at some time – a luncheon (or dinner) and a ball.

I would like to start by talking about these events because, as you'll see, you'll be able to pick up a number of tips which can be applied to many other fund-raising gatherings.

The fund-raising lunch

Not every fund-raising organisation will warrant an event of the size I describe overleaf, but the same principles will apply to even the smallest luncheon or wine and cheese party or charity picnic – you've still got to make it work, at a price you can afford, *and* make a profit.

A taste of her own medicine

Beware of members who get carried away at events, or your guest of honour could end up in hot – or, rather, cold – water, as Esther Rantzen did when she came along to present the cup at our 'It's a knock-out' at Fulham FC ground one year.

The presentation was to take place underneath one of the scoreboards, and unbeknown to anyone, while Esther was looking radiant in a red chiffon dress, Raymond Baxter and Richard Meade were climbing up a ladder at the back of the scoreboard with the intention of tipping a bucket of cold water over Eddie Waring, of Rugby League 'up and under' fame.

Unfortunately, though, they missed their target, and all the water fell on Esther Rantzen!

The girls on the scoreboard were very sweet and found Esther a change of clothing, but the good lady was not at all amused and left immediately after refusing my offer of a glass of champagne as a peace offering.

The next day I sent her a bouquet of flowers with an apology and persuaded the naughty boys, Messrs Baxter and Meade, to apologise likewise. They did so, reluctantly, because they maintained that the Esther Rantzen programme, *That's Life*, was based upon taking the mickey out of people and felt it was no bad thing for Esther to have had some of her own medicine.

By the way, I understand the BBC paid £200 for a new chiffon dress for Esther. But it was an unfortunate incident all round, not least because we upset a lovely lady who could have been of great use to us in the future.

Whatever the size of your charity, you have two problems when it comes to organising a charity lunch: getting bottoms on seats and then extracting money from the punters.

Ten things you must therefore do

1) Make every effort to obtain public awareness locally. Write to local business houses (find out the name of the chairman or managing director of the company and address your letter to him or her personally), and to your members (stressing the importance of selling tickets).

When you mail the initial letter it should say clearly what the funds are being raised for, and have a tear-off slip by way of an application form for tickets. And don't forget to put a closing date for application.

Try to sell tables rather than individual tickets (it makes life easier when you come to do the seating plan). Tables should be of ten to twelve – preferably twelve to maximise on space.

2) Select a venue that's the right size, accessible, and has a good reputation. Arrange to meet the banqueting manager and negotiate a 'charitable price' for the lunch. Bear in mind that the 'loading' you will place on the ticket (ie the profit your organisation will make on it) will be one of your major revenue contributions, so the better the basic price you negotiate, the higher the profit.

Don't forget that the hotel price will include gratuities and VAT which will have to be passed on to the purchaser of the ticket. The 'loading' will have to be a matter of judgment, depending on what you think the locals can stand.

There is little point in charging Savoy prices in Middle Wallop.

3) Find a tame printer who will offer you a special price for printing your tickets, brochure, etc. Make sure you give him the details he needs in plenty of time.

4) Look for a sponsor for the lunch. You can't expect him to pick up the tab for the lunch itself but if he gives you, say, £500, you can use it to buy a selection of wines for prizes.

Offer the sponsor a seat on the Top Table (sell him a table!). He can have a banner in the restaurant, his company logo on the menu, a tent card on his table and promotional literature for his company on the seats. He will also get a mention when the speeches are in progress. It's a very cheap way of advertising for him, so stress this.

5) Get a good speaker, it's the key to the success of your lunch. With respect, don't have your chairman — the vast majority of charity workers are beloved, blessed people, but on their feet would send you to sleep!

So you must never have a presenter who is selling your charity — even if it's your director — if he (or she) is dead boring.

(He will probably know he's a boring speaker, and if he doesn't, tell him!)

But you don't want to overdo it either; there's a balance for your credibility's sake. Clowning and one-line jokes are all very well, but you don't want the public to say, 'He should be on the stage, not telling us about the charity.'

If you can, try to get a celebrity whose name will help to sell the tickets, and get him or her to agree well in advance of the lunch so you can mention in your initial letter that he or she will be at your event.

There are a number of agencies who can provide you with a celebrity after-dinner speaker for a few hundred pounds (the sponsorship money could cover this if you get the wines donated).

The speeches should not last longer than thirty minutes — businessmen and women have to go back to work afterwards.

6) Arrange a bar extension.

7) Plan a '£5 lucky draw' for the wines. Remember that it is illegal to deface a coin of the realm so, although banks do accept money with names written on it, the best plan of action is to have a paper £5 voucher — design one and photocopy it — on which the donor writes his name, and which goes into the drum for the draw.

You can put as many vouchers as you like on the table to encourage donors to give more than five pounds. Our 'take', in fact, has gone up since we adopted this method — and complied with the law!

Provided you announce, 'We need your help for . . . because . . . this lunch is for you to give,' etc, at least 80 per cent of your guests should put in a fiver.

8) Consider making the lunch an annual event so that local

businessmen and women get used to the idea of supporting your cause at the same time each year. In this way, ticket sales should grow.

9) Entrust the task of choosing the menu to a woman on the committee, or the wife or girlfriend of one of your male committee members; in general, men are not particularly good at this sort of thing. Drinkable wines are also important.

10) Make sure the lunch runs to a strict timetable and that the speeches do not self-indulge by over-running. Ten minutes each is enough. Remember, busy people have other things to do.

Talking from experience

The Lord's Taverners hold a spring and Christmas lunch each year. When I first joined the charity in 1972 it was held at the Café Royal in London – 400 attended the Christmas lunch and 500 the spring. A good number by any standards.

Since 1980, we have had to leave the Café Royal (capacity 700) and move to the Hilton, where we sell 1,000 tickets every lunch!

So remember, learn to build on your success and do not necessarily abandon a project because it was not too well attended the first time around.

Organisation, planning and attention to detail is the name of the game.

Example of how to make a profit at a charity lunch

Income		Expenditure	
£500	From sponsor	£2,000	ie 200 lunches at £10 each inclusive
£2,850	Sale of 190 tickets at £15 each (£5 'loading')	£500	Speaker (sponsored)
		£50	Top Table wines
£800	£5 raffle (80% buying tickets)	£200	Print bill
£4,150		£2,750	

Net profit: £1,400 – which, for a small charity, would be a good return for the effort.

Our launch lunch

There are various ways of letting people know that there's a new fund-raising organisation in the area, and one of these is to have a lunch, as we do to launch our regions.

In Leeds recently, we appointed a local chairman who appointed a committee who invited businessmen. I got Jimmy Edwards and a few other celebrities and Yorkshire cricketers along, and we announced that we were holding the event at a hotel in Leeds.

You have to work fairly hard to get people to buy tickets to the lunch, but you don't have any finance – this kind of event is self-liquidating. And it *always* makes a profit. Ours, in fact, was a great success and we now have an established region in Yorkshire.

(By the way, although the event was just to get the show on the road, we made full use of the occasion to fund-raise. We never have a lunch without having a £5 lucky draw, which is simple to organise – all you need are some decent prizes, which should be donated, and an enthusiastic team of helpers.)

The fund-raising ball

The organisation of a fund-raising ball or dance requires a lot of pre-planning. The first two considerations are the time of year and the venue, both of which are dictated by local factors.

A summer ball is always worth considering, particularly if an attractive venue can be found. We hold ours in the autumn but try not to leave it too late in the year as there is an awful lot going on just before Christmas, and the less competition, the better!

The biggest fund-raiser
The biggest fund-raiser at a well-run ball is from advertising sales

in the souvenir programme. As I said earlier, more than half the total revenue from our ball comes from selling advertising space in the programme. So take the possibility of producing a souvenir ball programme seriously.

The souvenir ball programme committee
You will need a special committee to produce your souvenir programme. They should begin work at least nine months before the ball, and their first task is to produce a rate card – that is, to set the sale price for a page of advertising, and from there on, pro rata. Prices must be set according to what the local market will stand.

For example, if you are selling to local shopkeepers you cannot ask as much as running a West End ball and selling to, say, the Rank Organisation.

Remember, companies can offset their donations against tax.

You will need a conscientious individual to handle things with the companies and the printer. Someone has to produce the 'dummy' for the printer – ie the draft, showing what will go where etc – which involves dealing with the artwork (ie illustrations etc) and chasing up copy dates (ie deadlines).

Invoices have to be raised for advertisers and voucher copies of the programme sent to advertisers with the invoice after the event.

Someone will have to be responsible for designing (or finding a designer for) the front cover, and writing (or commissioning) a certain number of pages of editorial – which will need attractive photographs, suitably captioned.

You'll find more about programme and brochure production in Chapter 6.

A price to pay?
Whether you sell the programme or not is up to you. We give ours away on the principle that guests at the ball will be spending enough money already and it is a nice gesture to include the programme in the price of the ticket.

The advertisers' money, remember, should cover the print bill and make you a good profit.

Try to get your programme printed in return for a table at the ball.

The tombola

The tombola is another major fund-raising element of the ball. Like the souvenir ball programme committee, you will need a tombola committee working nine months or so ahead of the event, collecting prizes.

All prize-givers should receive a credit in the ball programme.

Although everyone enjoys a tombola, may I strike a note of caution concerning being too greedy. . . . No-one likes to buy an envelope full of blanks! Aim to see that everyone who spends five pounds gets a prize.

And try to insist upon accepting good quality prizes only – gain a reputation for being the fund-raising group that always produces a high-quality tombola. It is depressing to spend a fiver and to win only a can of warm beer; and people who know they can look forward to your tombola will be more likely to jump at the chance of attending your next event.

Attach importance to the way in which the prizes are displayed, too. If your prizes are good, make sure everyone knows it.

The gift of the gab

Both selling advertising space and collecting tombola prizes can only be done on a one-to-one basis – general mail-shots are a waste of time.

Your committees, therefore, should ideally consist of people who know companies at at least sales and marketing director level; and you won't find out whom your committee members know unless you ask them! So before you appoint your team, do just that – as they say, it's often not *what* you know, but *who* you know.

A personalised letter and follow-up telephone call or visit by a pleasantly convincing representative of your organisation is the best way to avoid your request being turned down.

Once your ball has become established, selling space and collecting prizes will become easier, so don't be discouraged in your first attempt.

Just the ticket

Ticket prices are, again, a question of what your local market will stand. The ticket price should include the meal, dancing and the cabaret – but not the wines.

Get the wine list from the hotel and include it in your order form to guests, asking them to order their wines direct with the hotel beforehand. Banqueting managers will appreciate this, and guests will not have to queue for the wine order when they arrive at the hotel.

Make sure that the signature on the order form for tickets is the same as on the application for wines. Otherwise the banqueting manager may be confused and set up another table – this has happened to us, with embarrassing results!

Gee, they gotta band!

Engage a band that can play to suit all tastes of popular music. Variety is the key. If you can afford it, you can hire two bands of varying styles.

Above all, choose a band who will keep the customers awake, not send them to sleep.

Union rules dictate that bands can only play for a certain period of time, so see that your running order (ie order of events) allows for them to have suitable breaks. The band will provide appropriate dinner music if desired.

If the band can accompany the cabaret (see below), all well and good. But most top carbaret artists will insist upon having their own accompaniment.

And don't forget – they all have to be fed and watered!

Come to the cabaret

The cabaret should not go on later than 11pm for two reasons: the artists don't like it and, later than that, the guests are inattentive. (The alcohol by then is taking effect!)

No cabaret should last more than forty minutes. Always leave your customers on a high rather than a low. The choice of cabaret depends upon the venue and the acoustics. Comics can die a death whereas a singer such as Barbara Dickson is always a hit.

If a top artist gives his services free for charity, don't forget that you will have to pay full rates for the accompanying band. Union rules do not recognise charities!

The toastmaster

The band and the toastmaster should each receive an 'outline programme' for the evening, with precise timings for the event.

It will be the toastmaster's job to see that the running order is carried out and kept to time. Nothing is worse than when a programme goes adrift because the cabaret has over-run, or the band has played for too long. Incidentally, the toastmaster usually has to be fed and the best time for this is during the cabaret or dancing.

The hotel should be able to get you a toastmaster; if not, you'll find a number of toastmasters, agencies and societies listed under 'Toastmaster' in the London telephone directory.

Don't let the toastmaster take charge of the event, though – he comes under your orders throughout the evening.

A smart affair

Most people like a black-tie affair – unless you prefer to choose something more 'down-market' but just as stylish, such as a flannel dance with boaters or a themed fancy dress event.

You should make it clear on the invitation that carriages are at 1 pm or whatever you decide. Impromptu extensions are not particularly popular and most guests will have already arranged for taxis home. Besides, the band will charge you extra!

Four things to remember

1) See that your committee sets out to make the evening fun, so that support will be forthcoming when you try it again the following year.

2) Don't lower your standards. A ball is hard work but with careful planning you can ensure it will be a success.

3) Make sure you have all the ingredients for success – that is, the right ambience, good food, good music, and a first-class cabaret.

4) Keep an eye on the clock.

A typical running order for a fund-raising ball

The Church-spire Fund Ball on Monday 4th November 1987 at the Ever So Good Hotel, Park Lane, London W1. 7.30pm for 8.30pm. Black tie.

TIME TABLE		ACTION
7.30pm	Reception	(Names of
7.30pm	VIP's reception, Park Suite	people
7.30pm	Tombola opens	responsible
8.10pm	Dinner call	should be
8.20pm	Dinner call to VIP's reception	inserted in this
8.30pm	President, chairman and guests proceed to Great Room	column – toastmaster,
8.35pm	DINNER	banqueting
9.30pm	After sweet/coffee: FIVE STAR SUPER DRAW ANNOUNCEMENT (Attendants will go round immediately to collect £5 vouchers with name and table written on them. Fourteen marvellous prizes, listed in programme and on back of menu)	manager, president etc)
10.00pm	Tombola reopens	
10.00pm	Dancing to the Ray McVay Show Band	
10.00pm	Behind stage: super draw takes place	
10.45pm	FIVE STAR SUPER DRAW WINNERS ANNOUNCED (Winners to collect prizes on balcony)	
11.00pm	Tombola closes	
11.00pm	THE CABARET	
11.40pm	Dancing resumes	
2.30am	National anthem	
2.30am	Carriages	

Get the batting order right

You should always be careful when arranging the order of speakers at a luncheon: I learned that the hard way, after making the most embarrassing faux pas at a Lord's Taverners' lunch.

By good fortune, I had been able to engage the services of the great impressionist, Mike Yarwood, who, I decided, should make the final speech of the event. The climax, if you like.

In fact, we had three speakers on that occasion, the first being broadcaster and cricket writer Christopher Martin-Jenkins – who, to my astonishment, stood up and delivered a terrific speech peppered with some excellent impressions of John Arlott and Alan Whicker. So successful was he that Mike Yarwood leaned across to me and said, 'Tony, this is a fix!'

Christopher Martin-Jenkins sat down to a standing ovation, a difficult act to follow for poor Mike Yarwood who I hope, by now, has forgiven me!

The moral of this story: if your first speaker gets a standing ovation, then you know you've got your batting order wrong.

8 · New Ideas and Old Favourites

Bright ideas and individual efforts

It's being creative that really gives me a kick – which is why I'm not going to waste any time talking about how to organise those basic bread-and-butter fund-raising schemes such as sponsored swims and slims (besides, I'm sure you already know how they work).

Instead, here are a few of the more unusual fund-raising ideas we've tried out at The Lord's Taverners, which have been successful and which have often spurred on our members to great ideas of their own.

By the way, just because we're a large charity, don't dismiss these ideas out of hand. Remember that, with a bit of flair, you should be able to scale down any large event to a size that can work for your own organisation.

The charity golf tournament

Golf is now universally popular and many charities are using this sport for fund-raising. A co-operative, well-located club, with good facilities and a good course, is imperative.

If you think a golf tournament is too ambitious for an organisation of your size, why not hold the event on a putting green or croquet lawn – the same principles apply.

The infamous Bob Hope Classic still leaves a nasty taste in the mouths of all fund-raisers – the expenses were so heavy that little more than 10 per cent of the 'take' went to the beneficiary. So be warned: don't let the size of your event get completely out of hand, and therefore out of control. And, above all, watch the expenses.

The players in our charity golf tournament consist of celebrities, amateurs and professionals in teams of four (two amateurs, one celebrity and one professional). Stewards for the course and all the golf administration is handled by members of the golf club, and the club is paid a fee for carrying out these duties since use of the course is denied to members that day.

The three ways of making money in a golf tournament
1) Sponsorship of the holes
Sponsors are invited to 'buy' a hole for the event. They can dress the tee with their commercial banners and logos; they can also have a marquee to entertain clients, and a page of advertising in the programme at half price.

They can nominate two players to play in the tournament alongside a professional and a celebrity – companies will pay a lot of money for the chairman to play with, say, Peter Allis or Sir Harry Secombe.

If you succeed in selling all eighteen holes (with no overheads) you should clear at least £10,000 from this aspect of sponsorship. Of course, in the really big events there is an overall sponsor, but for everyday charity promotion it is better to involve as many companies as possible. Putting all your eggs in one basket can be dangerous and I think it is more fun to have a series of mini-sponsors.

2) Gate money
If you have a good celebrity list of players the public will roll up in large numbers provided the event has been well advertised in the press and on local radio. I think that on a fine day there is nothing more pleasant for a family outing than to walk a beautiful golf course, watching the celebrities and professionals. My wife enjoys a Lord's Taverners' golf day and she is not particularly sporting minded.

It is a good idea to provide a further attraction near the clubhouse with refreshments and side shows. For little extra money the Red Devils or Police Dogs will give a demonstration to entertain the public.

A good public address system and commentator is essential. Also, an officials' caravan where players report for their start times, luncheon tickets, etc.

The efficient handling of tee-off times is vital if prize-giving is not to be delayed. For the public, it has been a long day and if there has been too much slippage you will be presenting the cup to an empty house in the dark.

3) Souvenir programme (advertisement sales)

For your souvenir programme you need a decent cover design and just essential editorial (ie a letter from the chairman, and a little information about the charity, etc). The rest will be advertising.

It is a good idea to use the centre page spread (ie the two pages in the middle) for a plan of the course with the sponsors' holes clearly marked (they like this!).

Of course, sales of programmes are not always very successful. 'Entrance by programme' is often better, with a 'loading' on the ticket. These days most members of the public arrive by car, so prices should take account of this. Try charging more for a car-load. If the entrance is £2, then it should be a fiver per car.

Some other golf ideas

If what I have outlined is on too grand a scale for your particular fund-raising operation, may I suggest some other ways:

1) Company Day ventures

Many companies have their own golf days on an annual basis. If you can, why not approach them with, say, three or four celebrities to play in return for a fee for your charity. This not only gives the company a good feeling by adding a charity flavour to a fun occasion, but also the prestige of introducing clients to well-known personalities.

Celebrities who like golf are often only too pleased to be associated with your charity in a Company Day venture.

We have prepared a leaflet which we send to selected companies inviting them to stage a golf day – your local golf club secretary will be able to tell you the names of companies playing on your home course.

The advantage of joining in with a Company Day is that the

company and the club do all the work and you only have to provide the celebrities for a fee. (Incidentally, if any company executives reading this would like a golf day for their organisation with celebrities involved – the money going to our charity of course – just give me a ring.)

2) A golf auction dinner
It's a good idea to hold a dinner the night before the tournament and get an auctioneer to 'auction' the players. A lot of money can be raised this way if you have the right punters present.

Taverners' Day

In 1985 I started our annual Taverners' Day, or Founders' Day, when each member was obliged to wear his tie and *contribute*: he had to do something innovative and of his own efforts.

The idea really caught on – challenging the members to concentrate their efforts on a specific day and with a specific aim worked wonders – and I'd recommend any charity or fund-raising group to consider something similar.

For those who needed some help – and you can't, unfortunately, expect all your members to be wildly imaginative – I sent out the following selection of ideas:

1) Find two covenanters of £250 per annum for four years (see Chapter 9)
2) Covenant yourself
3) Find ten people to become 'friends' of The Lord's Taverners
4) Hold a cocktail party on a pay basis
5) Hold a garage sale
6) Get yourself sponsored for a run, swim or weight-loss
7) Hold a local raffle
8) Donate funds from a professional engagement
9) Sell something valuable which you don't really want or need
10) Arrange a luncheon with a celebrity speaker
11) Stage a sporting event
12) Reach for the cheque book!

We got some fantastic results. One chum of mine, Colin Pegley, went round his home town collecting rubbish – he fixed it with the council that he would get so much per bag. Each sack he collected had to be weighed and handed into the council offices, and working from dawn to dusk he raised about £1,350.

Another chap took part in the Pamplona bull run in Spain – running in front of bulls down a cobbled street – and raised £1,000 from sponsors for his daring.

Other fund-raising ideas that year included: a tattoo contest, a jumble sale, a dinner party at the Hilton, a barbecue party, and a sponsored tennis event. Several people donated the fee for a professional engagement, while *my* contribution was to sell a boxful of cricket bats, each autographed by the England and Australian cricket teams, plus an assortment of twenty or thirty other famous personalities like Denis Thatcher, Harold Wilson, Colin Cowdrey and Peter May. The cost of the fifty bats was paid by a member.

The total raised that year was £25,000!

Cruising with the stars

The Lord's Taverners is probably the only charity that has done fund-raising afloat. Well, so far anyway. . . .

I persuaded P&O to engage a team of celebrities who, for a fee, would go on a selected cruise. 'Cruise with the Stars' helped P&O to sell tickets, and helped us to raise money – we had a captive audience of 1,800 people on the *Canberra* for a fortnight, all on holiday and all in a generous mood!

I suggested we have a daily event called 'Taverners Hour', between 5pm and 6pm, when we would raise money for our charity. Making the most of our celebrities, we did chat shows, panel games, a huge concert party, a sponsored walk around the deck etc. We collected around £8,000 and everybody – holidaymakers and celebrities alike – had a good time.

Smaller charities could consider asking a local sailing club or pleasure-boat company to let you go on board and collect money for your cause, perhaps providing a cabaret or raffle during a trip.

Or why not sell tickets for your own charity pleasure-boat ride? Hire a boat from Westminster to Richmond (or some other suitable stretch of river or canal) and have a fund-raising activity on board, with a couple of celebrities if you can get them.

And why stop at boats and ships? There's nothing to stop you operating the same kind of scheme on an excursion bus, inter-city coach or local sight-seeing tour — that is, if you can get the company concerned to agree. Even Concorde is for hire!

It's often the simplest ideas that are the best

Why not try giving a prize, sponsored of course, for the most innovative fund-raising idea? You'll be surprised what the most unlikely candidates will come up with. The local media will like it as well, which means extra publicity for your cause.

1) Prize-winning press-ups

A chap rang me recently and said: 'At three o'clock I'm going to do fifty press-ups in sixty seconds and I'm getting myself sponsored.'

I said: 'You must be mad at your age!'

He rang me at 3.30 and said: 'I did fifty press-ups in sixty seconds, then I did six more . . . and collapsed! And I raised £580.'

He has to be a contender for the prize I offer every year for an idea that has simplicity and practicality, and which everybody can adopt.

2) Remember the kids

Another simple but brilliant idea came in a recent letter from another member. It's called 'Remembering the kids'.

Basically, this chap suggested that every member should donate £5 for every healthy child in his family, and £2.50 for every healthy grandchild. It's nice, clean, and vaguely sentimental — and the response has been terrific, not to mention entertaining . . .

One man sent me a letter that said: 'Here's a cheque for £10 for my two children, and a cheque for £90 for all the others that I haven't been able to trace!'

One said he hadn't got any children so he was sending money for his neighbour's children, while another said he hadn't any children so he had counted his dogs.

But the best letter came from a chap who wrote: 'Remember the kids — how could I forget 'em? . . . Thought about sending them to you. But here's a cheque for £10 instead.'

An idea that never fails

At our cricket matches, we always get the corners of a blanket held by celebrities, and they go round the ground inviting people to chuck in their coins.

These 'blanket collections' always raise between £300–£500 with a reasonable gate of 2,000–3,000 people, without any trouble at all.

Worth thinking about, isn't it?

When the worst comes to the worst

The number of things which can go wrong at a fund-raising event are manifold, and I don't believe it pays to dwell upon them too much for your peace of mind!

However, they do exist, so remember the two things you must always do:

1) Keep calm
2) Have contingency plans

Plan in advance what you'll do if your guest of honour is late or fails to turn up, for example. Think what else could cause havoc and make sure you've always got something up your sleeve.

Here are a few of the unexpected things which have happened at Lord's Taverners' events – and what we've learned from them.

1) It's rained at an outdoor event

The Lord's Taverners have staged cricket matches where it has rained all day and not a ball has been bowled.

Sponsors, on the whole, are very good about Acts of God; provided everyone has turned up and you have obviously done your best to stage the match, they will be tolerant and give you the money. The answer is to ensure that there is an indoor facility if at all possible. In our case, celebrities have mingled with our sponsors' guests and at least the luncheon party has gone ahead.

(Incidentally, this happened to ASDA, the supermarket chain, in two consecutive years at a cricket match at Blenheim Palace. They were very good to us and coughed up the sponsorship money because every one of our players turned up and joined in the social side. They chose not to sponsor the match for a third year – and who could blame them? However, that year saw a brilliantly sunny day and was a great success for everyone else!)

2) There was no sign of the bus we were presenting

We had an occasion recently when we were presenting a 'NEW HORIZON' mini-bus to a home for the handicapped. The celebrity was standing with all the dignitaries, ready to make the presentation – but there was no sign of the bus! The driver had gone to the wrong address and arrived six hours late, which caused embarrassment all round.

There was very little anyone could have done about it at the time, but a sense of humour comes in handy on such an occasion.

3) We over-ran

There is nothing worse than staging an event which doesn't run to time. Apart from the chaos this can cause, it's also inconsiderate of the organisers of an event to ignore their guests' other commitments – no guest likes to have to creep out in the middle of a speech.

Your organisation will prosper if you build up a reputation for running to time, and nowadays I always try to see that if a lunch is advertised for one o'clock, we sit down at one o'clock on the dot. That's not always easy with 800 people present and many arriving late. But if you delay the start, the delay begins to compound itself.

It's very easy for even the most experienced speaker to over-run, so make sure you keep him or her tightly under control – don't let your speaker go over the allotted time because he or she feels that the audience is appreciative.

(By the way, your VIP speaker won't be too thrilled if you over-run and he's still waiting to do his bit when it's time for him to be wending his way home. I once took Ronnie Corbett to speak at a dinner of our region in Wales. He did not get to his feet until midnight, and was not best pleased with me – and I don't blame him! But the Welsh are a law unto themselves when it comes to public speaking . . .)

4) We lost momentum

I have noticed that at many events I attend, the master of ceremonies – or whoever is in charge – will announce a ten-minute 'natural break'. In my view, this is a mistake.

If anyone wishes to spend a penny, they'll do so unobtrusively; if you organise a mass exodus, the whole evening, like a soufflé, will sag – and what was once a high point will become a low point.

A seasoned audience will very quickly see whether the chairman of the evening has a firm grip on affairs, and the running order in particular.

5) We had a boxing match – with no ring

Ten years ago I staged a Henry Cooper Boxing Evening.

Picture the scene: a packed room of 900 spectators at the Royal Lancaster Hotel in London; boxing – Young England versus international opponents; celebrities including Henry Cooper, Harry Secombe and Freddie Trueman, who are sitting at the Top Table. The boxing is about to start and there's an air of expectancy and excitement. But one vital ingredient is missing – the boxing ring!

Ever felt foolish? I've got 900 people, boxers and ABA officials staring at an empty square in the middle of the room.

It transpired that the lorry bringing the ring had broken down on its way to the hotel and the only thing I could think of doing was to keep calm and ask if there was an AA official in the audience. Imagine my surprise when the Head of Operations at the AA came forward. He was magnificent: he contacted the AA on his intercom and managed to get the ring delivered within the next hour. It was then assembled by some wonderful hotel staff in thirty minutes.

Contingency plans? I did consider announcing a cabaret involving Harry Secombe and Freddie Trueman, but luckily it didn't get that far. Just as well, really – our good friends Secombe and Trueman were sweating blood!

6) No-one bothered to tell me an idea had been dropped

I am often approached by promotional companies with bright ideas. However, very often the scheme they're proposing has not been properly worked out and agreed with the company concerned.

For example, a few years ago, I was visited by a chap who was doing a sports competition for Total, the oil company. His idea was presented to me as if it were signed and sealed: all I had to do was to raise prizes for sports competitions in the form of 'A day at the Harry Secombe Golf Classic', 'A game of cricket with the Lord's Taverners', etc.

In the sailing category I suggested, 'A day out in *Morning Cloud*' – Edward Heath's yacht – which was regarded, quite rightly, as a plum.

In order to achieve this, I called upon Edward Heath, a Lord's Taverner, at his home. The great man was charming and readily agreed to place his famous yacht at our disposal for a prize.

Days and weeks went by and I eventually found out that Total had decided to drop the whole scheme. No-one had bothered to tell me, and I was left having to apologise for wasting everyone's time. Nugatory work, I think it is called.

So beware of promotional companies with bright ideas, and insist upon the deal in writing before taking action.

7) We put in a lot of effort for little return

It's very difficult to run a successful horse-race charity event. The Variety Club do it because they've got the key course and every year they make a lot of money. But we've never raised very much at a race meeting.

The organisation involved is enormous and the scope for making money is limited. First of all, you have to raise a large amount to get the sponsors for the runners, and you must raise a decent amount of prize money to attract a good field. So you need at least £12,000–£15,000 for the jockeys who will go in for the race, and the prize money has got to be attractive.

If you don't get a decent field you won't get a decent turnout to watch, and if you don't get a decent turnout you don't get decent gate money. It really is a bit of a nightmare.

The social entertainment is also rather up-market as against the fund-raising. Everyone expects to splash champagne around, so expenses are high. And racecourses aren't too keen on giving their courses for charity race meetings anyway. You can't even rely on the gate money to be a money spinner, particularly if the weather's foul.

The moral: avoid a horse-race charity event unless you secure a very generous sponsor and can be sure to make a lot of money on the race card (programme).

Flag days and street collections

I have run several flag days for Brian Rix and the Friends of Normansfield who support a home for the mentally and physically handicapped, and have discovered that the money you raise is in direct proportion to the manpower you can organise: the more box-shakers you have, the more money you will raise.

That is the crux of the problem. It is no easy matter to find volunteers to stand for, say, three hours on a street corner shaking boxes to an indifferent public. But this is what has to be done, regardless of the weather, too.

Five things you need to know about flag days

1) To hold a flag day you need to get permission from your local council. Applications should be made twelve months in advance and a Saturday is your best bet. Councils have a limited number of days to set aside for collections.

2) The Home Office stipulates that all collectors must be issued with a certificate and badge supplied by HQ. Both must carry the name and address of the collector and be signed by the organiser.

Tins must be sealed, numbered and entered on a special form together with the name and address of the collector, and must be opened in the presence of the organiser and a referee – the amount collected entered on the form.

3) You must inform the police that you have a permit from the licensing authority. Street collections in London require the approval of the Metropolitan Police.

4) It is illegal to solicit money. So, I'm afraid, the collector will just have to stand there with a sweet smile on his or her face.
But you can shake the box like crazy!

5) The average box full of relatively low denomination coins will raise about thirteen pounds, so you have to shake a lot of boxes to raise, say, £5,000.

Making the most of flag days

1) Be sure to have an up-to-date local map, with the key areas marked off – ie busy shopping areas and suitable locations for collection points.

2) Give sufficient thought to the most effective places to position people – such as in and around pubs at lunchtime if you can get the publicans' permission, outside sporting events (but remember to choose your football ground wisely or your collectors could end up getting mugged!) and around tourist attractions and railway or bus stations.

3) Try and get co-operation from your local big stores, who may let you set up shop in their foyers. This is particularly helpful in bad weather – people are more likely to stop and open their purses in a warm shop than in a cold street. It's important to convince the store managers that you won't block their doorways, though.

4) Try and enlist the help of local voluntary services and/or the Rotaract and Round Table. All these organisations are contactable through your local authority, and they may provide helpers for you.

5) Make sure you've got adequate transport, manpower resources and equipment.

6) You'll need an HQ and local collection centres, which will have to be manned continuously.

7) Accountability is most important, particularly with flag days. Local banks can be most co-operative by looking after the money for you and in some cases providing helpers. You'll need a treasurer whose responsibility it is to see that all the funds are properly accounted for and publicly declared.

A list should be made of the amount in each tin and the name of the collector to whom it was issued. Returns should be made to the local authority on the appropriate form within a month of holding the flag day.

8) Pay attention to pre-publicity. It helps enormously if the local townsfolk are aware of what's going on; the press and local radio will always be only too pleased to help. If you can get one or two well-known names and faces to front your flag day, all well and good.

And on the day, why not tour the area in a specially decorated loudspeaker van, drawing attention to your cause?

9) Remember to announce in the press the total raised – try a letter to the editor.

10) Write and thank the helpers individually. They'll deserve the thanks – and, besides, you never know when you'll need them again.

Five things you need for a flag day
1) Collection tins (numbered and sealed)
2) Cardboard trays for flags (those with pins and the adhesive variety)
3) Flags or adhesive stickers
4) Collectors' badges
5) Posters to hang on the trays (to advertise your charity)

All the items listed above (with the exception of the posters) can be obtained from Angal Products, 48a Holmbush Road, London SW15, who are Britain's leading suppliers of cash-collecting equipment. Send for their catalogue which shows their range of collecting boxes, seals, emblems, dispensers and holders etc.

Don't forget – many collecting boxes can be placed in static positions such as in pubs. But remember where you left them!

A case for door-to-door collections
If you can find a sufficiently large labour force, local door-to-door collections can be very profitable. It depends upon the size of your organisation and whether you are set up on a regional basis throughout the country.

In my local town of Tunbridge Wells, for example, where we live on an estate, we are constantly having little envelopes pushed through the letterbox, which are collected the following week.

It is hard not to give when you are presented with the appeal on your doorstep.

Raffles

Lotteries is the generic term for raffles and other similar money-raisers. They've always been one of the easiest ways of raising money and are the stock-in-trade of most charities.

The main appeal of lotteries is that, though they are labour intensive and time-consuming, they don't require much pre-planning. But the Gaming and Lotteries Act imposes stringent rules, and you must study them beforehand.

In general terms, lotteries can be divided into entertainment, private and registered lotteries – and each has its own set of rules.

Entertainment lotteries

These require no registration and are suitable for dances, fêtes and other small occasions, when you want to raise a few quid with the minimum of fuss.

The rules are:

1) Tickets cannot be pre-sold and the result has to be announced at the function.

2) The purchase price of the prizes must not exceed £50 in total and there must be no cash prize. There's no restriction, though, on the ticket price.

3) Except for the printing of tickets, no promotional expenses are allowed, and there can be no public advertising.

(Normally, printing tickets is a waste of money – you can buy coloured cloakroom tickets from any reputable stationer's, in books of one thousand.)

Private lotteries

These also need no registration and are designed for societies or clubs and those at work under the same premises. Unlike entertainment lotteries, cash prizes are permissible as well as expenses which are limited to printing and prizes.

Again, no advertising, except 'in house'.

Registered lotteries

This is the most complex category and involves lotteries where tickets may be sold to the public.

By law, lotteries requiring registration are sub-divided into two categories:

1) Where the total value of tickets to be sold does not exceed £5,000
You must register with a local authority for an annual fee.

Organisers can then run lotteries fifty-two times per calendar year.

Ticket prices are limited to 25p and prizes may be in cash or kind – but the total value may not exceed one half of the proceeds. No single prize may exceed £1,000 in value, and expenses may not exceed 25 per cent of the whole proceeds.

Returns to the local authority must be made not later than the end of the third month after the date of the lottery.

2) Where the total value of tickets to be sold exceeds £5,000
A double registration and fee is required here, with both the local authority and The Gaming Board for Great Britain (address: Africa House, Kingsway, London WC2).

The latter registration covers:

a) *Short term* lotteries up to £20,000 (held more frequently than once a month). Prizes not to exceed £1,000;

b) *Medium term* lotteries up to £20,000 (held more frequently than once every three months but not more frequently than once a month). Prizes not to exceed £1,500;

c) *Long term* lotteries up to £40,000. Prizes not to exceed £2,000.

The organisers' name has to be printed on all tickets, and the Gaming Board can call for accounts which should be submitted within six weeks from the closing date of the lottery.

Example: The Lord's Taverners run an annual raffle, generally with Lanson champagne as the central prize. We begin selling tickets in August and make the draw at our Christmas lunch. Everyone likes to win a case of champagne at Christmas and we usually raise £5,000 each year from this popular event.

Raffle prizes

While you're selling tickets on the emotive nature of your charity, at the same time you have to titillate the punters on the human side by saying, 'You stand to win a holiday for two in the Bahamas, or something, so why not wager a five pound note against it?' If there were only 200 people in the room, that would seem a good deal to me.

The answer, therefore, is to try and get as attractive prizes as possible and announce what they are. But don't make the emphasis for your appeal on the prizes – it should be on the emotive nature of the charity. So tell them about your objectives.

I think it's very offputting to have a string of prizes. I personally don't give more than three or four, which I feel is quite adequate. Also, if they're much of a muchness, I don't give first, second, third and fourth prizes. The first person comes up and I say, 'There are the prizes, you pick.' So number four is the only one who doesn't get any choice.

That's much better because sometimes, strangely enough, the chap would rather have the booze than the holiday, or would rather have the signed cricket bat than something else because he wants it for his son.

But the prizes should be of a decent quality, even though it's a nightmare every time to get the prizes donated.

The draw
On the assumption that people like to see personalities, you should stand up and say, 'Ah, there's Glenys Kinnock. Would you like to come up, Madam, and draw the first prize?'

We try and get a personality to draw the first prize. At the Henry Cooper Boxing Evening we have a different person presenting each of the prizes, and each one goes up into the ring to do so.

If you aren't fortunate enough to have a celebrity in your midst, of course, you must choose the most well-known or potentially useful guest – the chairman of a large local company perhaps (who'll appreciate the free advertising and may well decide to convince his or her fellow board members to support your cause in other ways in the future), or a prospective parliamentary candidate (who'll come in handy as a guest of honour when he or she reaches the House of Commons!).

The publicity
As with all fund-raising efforts you should aim to get as much publicity as possible. Never forget to publicise the results of your raffles by informing the media.

Even better, invite a local press photographer along to record the event for his or her paper – the photographer will appreciate a free meal and you'll appreciate the publicity.

Auctions

An auction is a good adjunct to a fund-raising occasion, but it is essential to have the following:

1) a good auctioneer, who does not go on too long but at the same time encourages the bidding – a well-known personality is ideal. If you can get hold of a local professional auctioneer, all well and good;
2) some decent prizes – a holiday for two in some exotic spot, or something like a video camera, is a good start;
3) some good punters – nothing is more embarrassing than an unsuccessful auction due to lack of bids;
4) helpers strategically placed in the room who can immediately clinch the deal with the punter. Cheques are acceptable if they are made out correctly – plastic money and IOUs are not. Helpers must be quite firm in obtaining the money before parting with the prize.

Three things to remember when holding an auction
1) Make sure the auctioneer has a good description of what is being sold. He cannot be expected to do a good sales job if he is not adequately briefed. If it is a painting, for example, see that it is properly displayed while the auction is in progress. Supply the auctioneer with a set of cards bearing information on each item being auctioned.
2) Make sure that the prizes are all printed in the programme for the evening so that the punters are forewarned of things to come.
3) The auction should not take more than 30 minutes in toto.

Interesting fact: The most generous group of people within the community, according to a recent Charities Aid Foundation survey, is made up of married women between the ages 35–44 and over 55, who are not employed and have large disposable incomes.

9 · Other Money-making Schemes

Attracting donations

While most people undoubtedly derive much satisfaction from participating in the running of fund-raising events, you may not always have sufficient manpower to raise the money you need.

There are, however, a number of excellent fund-raising schemes which can be administered from your office and may well turn out to involve more in the way of organisation than effort.

The following schemes all involve attracting donations from companies and/or members of the public. For them to work you must adopt a professional, hard-nosed and aggressive approach – just as you would for any business enterprise.

Whichever you choose, aim high!

Covenants are worth considering

Covenants are the most cost-effective way of fund-raising. For every £10 of covenanted money you receive from the Great British public, the Inland Revenue will give you a further £4.28.

The only rules of the game are that:

1) you persuade the donor to make payment under a Deed of Covenant. This ties him in to supporting your charity for a minimum period of four years;

2) in order to reclaim his tax, you make sure he completes a form with the appropriate wording. Name, address, then the declaration: 'I, . . ., undertake to pay x each year for four years (or

during my lifetime if shorter) from today the sum that will, after the deduction of income tax at the basic rate, be £.....p.a.' It must be dated, signed and witnessed. Company covenants should have a company seal on the document;

3) in addition to the covenant form, you get a bankers' order signed by the donor with the first payment on the same date as the date of the covenant. This will be followed by three further payments on the same date for the next three years, if it is to be a four-year covenant.

Tax relief

Provided the donor pays tax at the basic rate, the charity reclaims his tax from the Inland Revenue. If the donor pays tax at a higher rate, he can claim higher rate relief, thereby reducing the cost of his donation.

Tax relief can also be obtained in single payments through a loan covenant. All the donor has to do is to sign three forms – a letter of loan, a Deed of Covenant and a waiver in the event of death.

Make sure that all the forms are signed before payment is made into your bank. Otherwise, tax relief will be jeopardised.

USEFUL TIP: Pre-printed forms ready for signature make light work of the administration. They are also a confident sign that you mean business!

USEFUL BOOK: 'Covenants' by Michael Norton, from the Directory of Social Change, Radius Works, Back Lane, London NW3 1HL. At the time of writing this costs £4.95.

Obtaining covenants

Though the rules of covenanting are fairly simple, be warned that obtaining covenants is not as easy as it sounds. Nevertheless, I do advise charities to go out and get covenants. From experience I would tell you that having gone through the blood, sweat and tears of finding a covenanter, it is then a great pleasure to sit back and watch the same amount of money roll in each year. And remember that four years is only the minimum period: covenants can be for seven and beyond. Wonderful if you can get them.

Selling the idea

Make no bones about it, covenanting is a selling job. People, therefore, must believe in your cause – and it's up to you to make sure that's the case.

Don't forget that covenants can be individual or company. With many companies, covenants are still, unfortunately, in the hands of the chairperson, and if a chairman's wife is 'into' a particular charity already, don't be surprised if you find yourself having to try elsewhere.

Getting covenants is a one-to-one business. You have to sit down with the person responsible – maybe even buy him or her a drink – and say, 'It's very kind of you to give me ten minutes of your valuable time'. Then you've got to explain your cause quickly and succinctly in plain, uncomplicated language.

In some cases, it is not easy to know who exactly is the decision-maker in a company. I have already suggested that it may be the chairperson. On the other hand, there is a tendency now to take the decision-making away from the board and give it to the marketing director who probably also looks after sponsorship.

From a company's point of view, this is a sensible move. But bear in mind that the marketing director is likely to be hard-nosed and, quite rightly, ask: 'What's in it for us?' or 'What are you going to do for my company?' 'How are you going to promote my company's sales?'

This tough approach is fair enough when there are so many worthy causes around to support, and you have to be prepared to answer these questions even though covenants, ostensibly, are not supposed to carry any benefit to the donor.

Getting your man – or woman

Begin by ringing up the chairperson's secretary. Ask who handles charitable trusts in the company, and make an appointment with him or her. When you go along, take with you your last year's audited accounts as well as a leaflet about the charity, or whatever other presentable information you have.

Find out if the company has been involved with your charity before and whether you have any local activity which may reflect upon the company – for instance, you may have a celebrity golf tournament coming up in the area where the company is active, and it may wish to promote itself by sponsoring a hole or taking a marquee for client hospitality.

It is worth noting that if you are going to a local company as a local branch of a charity you may get the brush-off because they already contribute to the charity via headquarters. So find out first.

Remember the adage, 'Time spent on reconnaissance is never wasted'.

You should also bear in mind that company boards do not always like covenants as a principle as it ties in the board's successors to lots of money without any say in the matter. The 1980 Finance Act, however, reduced the minimum period of covenants from seven to four years, which has helped the selling job enormously.

Getting support

Treasurers of charities are not always keen on covenants because of the amount of administrative work involved. But the rewards can be enormous. The Lord's Taverners, for example, raise £100,000 a year through covenants.

Always stress the advantages to both the benefactor and the beneficiary. The Chancellor's recent budgets have made life easier for all parties. New legislation includes:

1) specific VAT exemptions for goods or services supplied to certain charities and disabled persons;

2) companies (other than close companies) may obtain corporation tax relief on one-off payments to charities made under deductions of tax, subject to a limit of three per cent of their ordinary dividend payments, effective from 1 April 1986;

3) four-year covenants continue but the £10,000 upper limit on payments qualifying for higher-rate relief is abolished;

4) employees may, with their employers' consent, arrange for up to £120 per annum in charitable donations to be deducted from their pay with the benefit of tax relief (see page 115);

5) deduction of basic rate of tax from covenants to charities is now mandatory if relief is to be obtained.

The Treasury wants to classify charities but this idea, at the time of writing, is coming under fire from the Charity Commissioners and others who do not classify charities. It is likely that the Treasury will bow to pressure and abandon classifications. The proposed legislation was designed to catch out those with fraudulent intent.

Renewals

Remember that the sales pitch for renewals is more difficult than the initial one. There is only one cake, and many demands for a slice. So you have to be particularly smart to obtain a renewal.

Six months before renewal, I write and say, 'Your covenant has been an enormous success . . . with your money we have been able to do this, that and the other; its continuance is vital if we are going to continue with the good work etc. Will you please renew?'

Do everything you can to make the covenanter feel part of the team and stress that without his help much of what your organisation achieves would simply not be possible.

You should aim to get at least 50 per cent renewals provided you are actively seeking new covenants. I never cease to be amazed at the number of charities who do not bother about covenants at all.

Getting covenants is hard work and persuasion plays a prominent part in the sales process. But remember, the Government is keen on them — and so should you be.

Business is business

We've got a scheme where all our businessmen have to covenant, which is a good thing since the origins of The Lord's Taverners were *purely* thespian — members such as Laurence Olivier and John Mills were recruited by others who went round to stage doors and signed up actors on the back of an envelope!

Then television became a way of life and many TV personalities were recruited. In fact, despite the nature of our charity, The Lord's Taverners had around 200 members before they let any sportsmen in. (Naturally, the first to join were a number of famous cricketers.)

The members soon realised, however, that a great deal of administration was required to run an event — and with great respect to these marvellous showbiz people, they're not the greatest administrators. So the businessman crept in, eventually to such an extent that there was an imbalance between biz and showbiz. Showbiz revolted so we had to control the influx of biz!

Now we make the businessman covenant his membership. He has to pay £250 a year for four years, and on payment of his first £250 he automatically becomes a member of the Patrons' Club. It's virtually a club within a club, and members have a club tie and a meeting once a year. The businessman then becomes eligible to become a full member of The Lord's Taverners: he can be proposed and seconded as a member just like everybody else — so he's really bought his way in, if you like.

A lot of people have objected to this, but my view is, 'At least he has put his money where his mouth is.' I find that the calibre of the covenanted member is generally higher than that of the guy who came in because he was a friend of old Snodgrass, whom he met in the pub. That's how it was done in the old days — on an old-boy basis.

I'm not saying that everyone who joins has motives which are simply pure. It's a two-way thing; but I don't mind because if they think they're going to use me I'll make sure I get my pound of flesh out of them (£1,000 over four years, then they become members and have to pay a sub!).

Heads of PR companies are particularly keen on this idea. They think, 'Aha, now I'm going to have the entrée to Terry Wogan and David Frost, and can come to all the parties and rub shoulders with Jan Leeming.' If that's their motivation I don't mind at all — eventually I'll get hold of them and get them to sponsor something or do something in exchange.

Remember, though, that a covenant has to be given without any benefits in kind to the donor. The membership scheme, therefore, has to be treated quite independently. Membership is not an automatic reward or a result of covenanting. This would break the law of covenanting.

Legacies

Legacies, for one reason or another, are a much-neglected source of revenue for many charities – including my own. Yet the total legacy income obtained by all charities represents about 10 per cent of the total income.

I think this neglect is largely psychological. I'm not particularly disposed to asking my hale and hearty membership to leave something to The Lord's Taverners in their wills.

On the other hand, someone with terminal cancer is most likely going to leave a bequest or legacy for cancer research; someone with a heart condition may want to leave money to heart-disease research; while someone fond of animals may want to bequeath money to an animal charity – and the most amazing amount of money is left to animals!

Facts worth knowing about legacies

1) Gifts made to charities established in the UK are not subject to capital transfer tax, provided the gifts are applied for charitable purposes.

2) Some of the larger charities do actually run advertising campaigns for legacies. It is true that many benefactors are only prepared to give money to charities when they die, so why not cash in on this philosophy? Better late than never. (There is also, perhaps, an element of securing your place in Heaven!)

3) Solicitors who help people draw up wills often act as executors and thereby have powers to nominate your charity as a beneficiary. So it's often worth considering placing a charity advertisement in one of their yearbooks or journals.

4) Benefactors may leave money by general discretionary bequest to the Charities Aid Foundation, giving them a signed and dated memorandum setting out a choice of charities. There's no need for a formal codicil and donors may change their selection whenever they wish.

So be bold and resolute – not like me! – and ask your members and supporters to make a bequest on your behalf. They can only say no.

Give as you earn

In March 1986 the Chancellor of the Exchequer announced the introduction of The Charitable Deductions (Approved Schemes) Regulations 1986, whereby from 6 April 1987 business employees can arrange for deductions to be made from their salaries and given to the charity or charities of their choice. If just 10 per cent of the national workforce were to give one pound a week each by this method, a staggering £1 billion of new money would be raised for charity every year.

The main advantages
1) The deduction is made before calculating PAYE, which means that for somebody paying basic rate tax (27 per cent at the time of writing) for every £1 given to charity he or she would only be 73p out of pocket.

2) The charity in question is assured of regular contributions without the employee continually having to remember to reach for his or her cheque book.

Businesses will initially have an important part to play in the implementation of this scheme; they will have to decide, for example, with the help of an agency charity like the Charities Aid Foundation (CAF) – see below – the degree of choice.

The main features
1) The Inland Revenue will approve agency charities to run the schemes.

2) Approved agencies will make the necessary contractual arrangements with employers who wish to operate a scheme.

3) Employees who want to take part will authorise their employer to deduct their charitable gifts from their pay.

4) Employees can decide individually whether to support one or more charities of their choice, or may choose to elect a charity or group of charities en masse.

5) Employees can delegate to give all or part of their deduction to a committee, to be elected from the workforce.

6) The employer will make the deduction before calculating PAYE tax on the pay, effectively giving tax relief on the donation. The amount eligible for this tax relief will be limited — at present it is £120 per year.

7) The employer will then pay the donations to the agency charity.

8) An employer may encourage the choice of a charity or group of charities by offering to match employees' contributions, possibly by means of a four-year covenant.

9) The agency will act as a clearing house, distributing the donations to the individual charities to which employees wish their donations to go.

The Charities Aid Foundation
Established in 1924, the Foundation has enjoyed a long and successful history as a widely respected service organisation for charity. It currently acts as an agency charity for over 14,000 donors, distributing over £30 million of covenanted charitable donations each year. It also lists all the major charities as well as analysing charity figures, revenue, ratio of staff to funds raised, lists of grant-making trusts etc.

It was set up specifically to help and co-ordinate the raising and distribution of funds to other charities, and is used extensively by individuals and companies. They are provided with cheque books, and can donate amounts to any charity who then forward the cheques to CAF for payment.

The CAF simplifies the whole charity operation, making it easier for companies and individuals to give to charity, as well as giving a helping hand with covenant administration to nearly 300 individual charities.

What your fund-raising organisation must do
1) Take advantage of the scheme to approach businesses with attractive proposals. Like everything else, this is a selling exercise and should be treated with the same degree of professionalism as any other business venture.

2) Ensure that all approved agencies are aware of your existence and your aims.

What each business must do

1) Look at its payroll system and make provision for the payroll deduction. Many companies these days operate computerised payroll systems, and the deduction of pre-tax sums, once set up, is a routine function requiring no effort at all.

2) Consult the approved agency, who will take on most of the administrative donkey-work.

3) Present the scheme to the staff and begin talks between union and management where applicable.

It may be that employees choose to support a range of different charities, or they may vote to club together to support just one. Whichever is the case, the business must remember that it cannot dictate to its employees which cause they must support.

Further information

Businesses requiring information about this scheme should write to: Give As You Earn, Payroll Giving Services, Sterling House, 150–152 High Street, Tonbridge, Kent TN9 1BB.

The advantage of agencies

The use of agencies is a way of allowing some freedom of choice for employees without causing a great deal of extra work for employers or the Inland Revenue. At the time of writing eight charities have been approved by the Inland Revenue to act as agencies for company payroll giving schemes. Other applications are being processed. For an up-to-date list, contact the Charity Commission (see Appendix) or the address above.

An agency will have to fulfil the following requirements:

1) that its trust deed allows it to collect money from a public source;
2) that employee discretion is catered for, within reasonable limits;
3) that the through-payments go to charitable objects.

The Inland Revenue is in touch with a number of charity and employers' organisations about the administrative aspects of the scheme.

No government will ever have sufficient funds to provide sufficient services of a charitable nature. The new provisions will make it easier for the individual to establish the habit of regular giving.

A final note

It must be emphasised that employees have complete discretion over which voluntary organisation receives donations, even if association with a particular organisation is embarrassing for the company. Conversely, a health authority, for example, cannot dictate that employees contribute to its own trust funds.

It is also possible that trade unions will act as collecting agencies for their members.

Sponsorship

I have mentioned sponsors quite a lot in this book already but I make no apologies for that because sponsorship is the lifeblood of any charity, and often sadly neglected. Whatever the size of the charity, the less it actually has to pay for itself, the more it can give away.

Sponsorship is now big business, and you shouldn't be put off by the big battalions. There are plenty of potential sponsors on the market.

Many charity-minded companies, when dealing with smaller charities, regard their support as patronage rather than sponsorship and look for little reward or little return on their money invested in your event. But when you move into the big league and want some four-figure sums of money, the company you approach is going to want to know a bit more about you.

A sign of the times

In this day and age, it's unrealistic to think that every company is going to be motivated by charitable thoughts. And even if you find one that is, you're up against stiff competition – large companies, in particular, are inundated with requests for money; in addition, it's likely that a company's board members will each have pet charities they support, so when it comes to deciding which organisation gets the vote, you've got to have something more to offer.

You can't just go along with a begging bowl – you must take with you a promotional idea which will help the company as well as your organisation.

Be prepared

1) The first thing any responsible sponsor will wish to know is how much of your money actually goes in grant-aid. If he is to be allied with your work he is entitled to be satisfied that your fund-raising is cost-effective. *So watch those overheads!*

2) He'll then want to know whether his sponsorship will be high-profile or low-profile. That is, how much exposure his product will get. Will his company's name, for example, be included in the title of the event?

3) The vital question is, though, 'What's in it for us?' This is a perfectly reasonable question from a company.

As I've already mentioned, more and more companies are making their marketing directors responsible for sponsorship. And a marketing man will be looking to see how your event fits in with his marketing strategy. How, for example, can the occasion be tailored to promote a certain product?

The identity of milk with football in recent years is apposite. Drinking fresh milk as an association with keeping fit and participating in a virile sport is a natural.

4) Don't forget that the same principles will apply if you're a small organisation approaching a local shopkeeper. The sharper your idea, the more chance you'll have of getting something out of him or her. Remember, too, that however small the shop, this won't be the first time the shopkeeper has been approached by a charitable cause – so you've got to present him or her with an attractive package.

Advantages of sponsorship

1) To the company

a) A sponsorship package, properly organised, can be good news for a company seeking more public recognition.

The classic sporting example is the Cornhill Insurance Company, who had a very low profile before a certain gentleman in a rather scruffy raincoat walked into a friend of mine's office and said: 'Hello, I'm the assistant general manager of Cornhill . . .'

This pal of mine was asking for a large sum of money to save cricket, in the days of Packer, so that we could pay a retainer to the England side. And out of this meeting came the Cornhill sponsorship of all our Test matches.

Cornhill are now a household name. It appears underneath the scoreboard of every cricket match, so TV cameras can't fail to pick it up; they sponsor the England team, and regularly have promotions and receptions; and they also produce a Cornhill tie every year, which is worn by all the cricketers and commentators. All great publicity.

So there's a real success story, where the commercial gain has been substantial to a company.

b) There is also the consideration that working with a charitable cause can demonstrate a company's concern to be seen as part of the caring community. This is good for its local image, particularly if it has a factory in the area where the event is taking place.

If, for example, a company sponsors a Lord's Taverners 'NEW HORIZON' mini-bus, it will enjoy the sight of the bus driving around the locality bearing the company's logo. Press publicity for a local handing-over ceremony by a celebrity is also good PR for the company.

It's worth bearing in mind that sponsors working with a charity like to see their money being given to a charitable cause rather than being swallowed up in a charity's administrative costs and expenses. So if the beneficiary can be present at the event and be presented with a cheque by the sponsor, this will satisfy all parties.

2) To the charity

If a company becomes totally involved in your charity event, its own publicity machine will swing into action to promote the occasion. This can save your charity hundreds of pounds, because large companies tend to have their own promotional departments who can get behind your organisation and give it wide publicity.

Our own Harry Secombe Golf Classic, for example, was sponsored by the *Daily Express*. They have their own promotions department which handled all the publicity for this event, including the printing of the souvenir brochure, the sale of advertising and the production of car stickers and posters.

Besides, backed by a national newspaper, the event is bound to be brought to the attention of the public.

The big deal

No two sponsorship deals are alike, and each will be dealt with by the company on merits.

When negotiating a sponsorship, try to present your case in a sufficiently professional manner to obtain anything longer than a one-year sponsorship – ideally at least three. Continuity can be good for the company, and obviously helpful to you.

The sponsorship search is hard enough, so when you've found a sponsor, hang on to him.

One of the major problems of sponsorship is fixing a sensible fee for the event. Don't be too greedy when agreeing a figure – rest assured that the marketing director will have a good idea of how much he's prepared to pay. He'll also know that if his company becomes totally involved he can add 100 per cent on to the sponsorship fee for the promotional costs alone.

Sponsor tips

1) Beware of sponsorship and TV – it is not always good news for the sponsor unless the event bears his name. Even if you do succeed in getting your event televised, your sponsor should be under no illusions concerning the strict rules operated by the BBC.

For seven years, The Lord's Taverners participated in a full-blown celebrity knock-out with the full BBC team, including Stuart Hall and Eddie Waring. We provided a celebrity team in return for a fee from the BBC, and then we sold the event to a sponsor who naturally assumed he would be getting his name in lights throughout the programme.

The very opposite happened. Every time the sponsor put up a banner, the BBC told us to take it down. It was a constant battle, and each year we gained a little something for the sponsor, but it was an uphill struggle all the way.

Producers and editors on BBC television throughout the country have now been told that they must 'contain' any promotional material associated with sponsorship to an absolute minimum.

So don't think you can offer your sponsor his name in lights, because you can't. The BBC will hound you to death!

2) Be careful of overkill. If you have a friendly sponsor who has been good to you, don't skin him alive! It is so often the soft option to go back to the same guy, but it is kinder – and in the long run,

more beneficial – to ring the changes.

But by all means put him on your mailing list and, if you have a covenant scheme, invite him to become a covenanter.

3) Even though you're a charity, it is not at all improper to spend a little money entertaining your sponsor. If you have a well-known name fronting your charity, get him along too – even company chairmen like to rub shoulders with the high and mighty.

4) Don't ever take a sponsor for granted, and don't forget to say a warm 'thank-you'. We hold an annual reception for sponsors only, so that our president can thank them personally for their help for the charity during the year. Believe me, this is very much appreciated.

We also present all our sponsors with a Lord's Taverners plaque as a memento of the occasion, and we try to invite them as guests to other events.

Above all, we make it abundantly clear that we regard them as the lifeblood of our charity.

5) Take sponsorship very seriously. We have a Sponsorship Committee whose job It is to attempt to come up with sponsors for our various events throughout the year. Including our regions, we have to find at least one hundred sponsors each year. Members of the committee, therefore, need to be of marketing director level, with a wide range of contacts.

See that each event has a clearly written brief from which your committee or the person responsible can sell – nothing is worse than to have an interested sponsor and an insufficient brief for him.

6) Study the stock market and business news. There is no point in approaching companies who are struggling for survival. Even stockbrokers were known to be giving away money to charity after the pre-tax profits they made at the sale of British Telecom!

Another interesting fact: financial institutions are way ahead of other business categories in the top two hundred corporate donors, followed by food, alcohol and tobacco companies.

Keep your eyes and ears open

When reading newspapers and magazines, watching TV or listening to the news, always be on the lookout for anything you can turn to your own advantage. For example, you might hear of a well-known person who supports your kind of organisation, or a company who might want to be associated with your cause, or even a celebrity who has just moved into your area and might like to be guest of honour at one of your events.

Here are two occasions when I've turned something I've learned from the media to our advantage. . . .

1) When Archer was bowled over

A year or so ago, I was watching Jeffrey Archer being interviewed on television. He was talking about his love of cricket (of which I had no idea), and in particular his admiration for Ian Botham who then played for Somerset (Jeffrey Archer's county). He also mentioned that he lived in Rupert Brooke's old house, The Vicarage at Grantchester near Cambridge.

Armed with this gratuitous information, I wrote to him at Grantchester inviting him to speak at our next spring luncheon in London – where I promised him he would be able to sit next to his cricket hero, Botham. The bait was too great for Jeffrey Archer and I was delighted to receive his prompt acceptance.

2) When a company went cricket crackers

In November 1985 I read an article in *The Times* concerning the activities of Hovells, the Christmas cracker manufacturers, who had just taken over another company.

I wrote to Hovells and asked if they would provide crackers for the one thousand guests who would be attending our Christmas luncheon in December. The company very kindly said yes, and we were able to provide a colourful touch to the event at no cost to the charity.

Charity trading

Many charities will find themselves trading in the commercial sense. This is perfectly OK provided:

a) the trading is irregular;
b) you are not competing with other traders;
c) public support is substantially because all the profits are for charity.

Provided these conditions are satisfied, the Inland Revenue will not worry you, particularly if the goods are donated or in tombolas etc.

As in all things, moderation is the key. If trading assumes such proportions as to render it a dominant purpose of the institution, then the Charity Commissioners and the Inland Revenue will be down on you like a ton of bricks.

If you want to trade on a permanent basis then the Commissioners advise you to set up a non-charitable trading company in order not to endanger your charitable status. Such a trading company may be wholly owned by the associated charity or owned jointly by several charities.

All profits to the charity from the trading company are best paid by a Deed of Covenant in order to avoid paying corporation tax. The Inland Revenue will advise on Deeds of Covenant.

Buying and selling tips

1) Most charities have their own little lines for trading with members and the public – things like bookmarks, key rings etc. But, for heaven's sake, don't order too much. Only order as much as you can sell. I order in minimum quantities. There is no point in getting a reduction for bulk if you cannot shift it.

2) There are a number of promotional gifts companies (they're listed in Yellow Pages) who will produce ideas for charities to sell. They will often hold the stock and sell it for the charity by making a handling charge which is passed on to the customer.

3) If you find some of your stocks are not moving, be a devil and have a sale.

4) Although the funds from the sale of your goods are going to

charity, do not be too greedy. If you make a modest and sensible mark-up on your goods, you are more likely to sell a large number.

Don't forget
Charity trading must *not* dominate your fund-raising operations. If it does, then you must set up a private trading company – and for this you would be well advised to consult a solicitor who specialises in charity affairs, as it can become rather complicated.

Card sharp

A popular form of charity trading is the charity Christmas card. Each year, many large charities have cards specially printed which they sell to make money for their cause. In fact, of the one billion Christmas cards sold annually, roughly a quarter are charity cards.

But before you embark on this project you've got to think about your market – what kind of cards your members are likely to buy, how much they'll be prepared to spend, how many cards you're likely to be able to sell.

As I've said earlier, to make a profit you must only produce as many as you feel confident you can sell, even though this may cost more initially. Unlike other lines, Christmas cards must be sold at a particular time of the year; and left-over cards, even at a bargain price, will be hard to shift until later the following year.

In addition, you must remember you'll have to have somewhere to store unsold cards – particularly important if you grossly over-order.

Designs on money-making
The simplest and cheapest way to produce a Christmas card is to invite an artistic local person to do a simple cover design for you – ideally free of charge. The fewer colours he or she uses in the design, the cheaper the printing costs will be. But be careful that the card doesn't look 'amateurish'. It must look sufficiently professional to compete with the ever-increasing numbers of attractive Christmas cards on sale in local shops.

Another way of saving money is to buy cards through the Charity Christmas Card Scheme (Radius Works, Back Lane,

London NW3 1HL). You'll share designs and print costs with other charities – only the wording of the message inside, and the name of your organisation, will be different.

If you're a large organisation, you might be able to interest local businesses to buy your cards, with their own name overprinted. For this, you'll have to offer a larger card, and maybe a selection of designs.

The sell out

To make sure all your members buy some cards – and, hopefully, sell some to their friends as well – you must make sure they know about them in plenty of time. That means organising their production well in advance, publicising your intentions well, and putting the cards on sale *just* as people are thinking of buying their Christmas cards – *not* after they have already bought some!

Without a huge membership, though, you won't make much money unless you consider other ways of selling your stock. Try your local Council for Voluntary Service, which may run a charity card shop on a temporary basis just before Christmas, selling cards in aid of local charities; ask local shops if they would be prepared to display and sell your cards (you must expect to offer shops a discount of around 20–25 per cent); or consider taking a stall at a Christmas bazaar.

A final thought

Before you try Christmas cards as a means of making money, be certain it really is.

USEFUL ADDRESS: The Charity Christmas Card Council (4Cs), 49 Lambs Conduit Street, London WC1N 3NG. They organise a scheme whereby your cards can be illustrated in a catalogue they send out to a large number of companies.

USEFUL BOOK: 'Charity Christmas Cards: How To Produce Them, How To Sell Them, How To Make Money Out Of Them', available from the Charities Advisory Trust, Radius Works, Back Lane, London NW3 1HL. At time of writing, price £3.95.

Nothing for nothing

If your organisation gets a 'freebie', don't just give it to a committee person or councillor as a reward for all his or her hard work. Think how you can use the situation for fund-raising.

In 1983, for example, we were enormously privileged to be invited to dine at 10 Downing Street, where the Prime Minister was going to host a dinner for The Lord's Taverners.

When I announced this tremendous invitation to the council – our governing body – they naturally all assumed that they would be invited as a reward for the work they'd done. But instead I said I thought the Prime Minister would expect us to make some effort to fund-raise for that particular occasion, which automatically ruled out all the council. It was a great disappointment to them, but not to the charity.

In fact, what we did was invite thirty couples to pay for the privilege of dining at No 10. The price? – £1,000 a year, covenanted for four years. With that money I was able to buy a whole lot of mini-buses.

It was a most memorable evening, but out of it came help for those in need.

A good investment

If you've raised large sums of money, it makes good financial sense to earn interest on it rather than simply leave it sitting in a bank current account. Remember that as a charity you are tax exempt, and you will not pay tax on interest you earn on your investments.

But before you make an investment (other than in a bank deposit account or money fund) you are obliged to seek professional advice in writing under the 1961 Trustee Investment Act.

There are three kinds of investments: short-term, medium-term and long-term.

Short-term investments

Short-term generally implies the need to withdraw within, say, seven days. In this respect, you would consider the following:

a) bank deposits – these pay a relatively low rate of interest but are convenient as automatic transfers can be made from your current account;
b) money funds – these are investments made on the money market with a higher rate of interest than bank deposit accounts. There is generally a minimum deposit of about £2,500. (Save and Prosper are one of the specialists in this form of investment);
c) building society accounts – these usually require seven days' notice of withdrawal and there's no minimum deposit. Interest is paid net of tax and charities then have to reclaim the tax.

Medium-term investments

This is suitable if you have money which isn't required for at least one month. National Savings offer higher interest rates on deposits up to £200,000 at one month's notice of withdrawal. You can also invest in Government stocks designed to mature at about the same date that you will need the money.

Long-term investments

If you have long-term funds for investment, such as your reserve fund, then you are strongly advised to consult the experts. Make a note of two such bodies who help charities:

1) Charities Official Investment Funds (COIF), 77 London Wall, London EC2N 1DB;

2) Official Custodian for Charities, 57 Haymarket, London SW1Y 4QZ.

The latter will hold your securities, deal with registration and reclaim tax on your behalf on the dividends, free of charge.

There are, of course, well-known companies in the City who will look after charity investments, in all the aspects I have described, free of charge.

Your reserve fund

Don't be shy about building up a substantial reserve fund for contingencies. All reputable charities have reserve funds capable of sustaining them when the going is hard or there is a large capital expense to be faced up to – such as the purchase of property.

There will always be pressure upon the governing body by members to disburse all their funds. But remember, you are the custodians for generations to come.

USEFUL LIST: 'Charities Listing', available from Building Society Choice, Riverside House, Rattlesden, Bury St Edmunds, Suffolk IP30 0SF (price £1), lists the best of the special building society accounts for charities. As usual, rates vary according to the sum invested and the notice required for withdrawal, but good returns are available even for small investments with easy access.

Government funding

You may be able to get a grant for your charity or fund-raising organisation from either your local authority or from central government.

Local authority grants
You don't have to be a registered charity to apply for a local authority grant but you *will* have to prove you are a non-profit making organisation providing a public service. These are the legal requirements under Section 137 of the 1972 Local Government Act.

Local committees serving local authorities may well, however, add additional conditions over and above the legal requirements, so it's up to you to find out from your authority whether it has any special requirements for eligibility. For example, some local authorities insist upon helping *only* registered charities and require audited accounts.

Government grants
Governmental grants are made by appropriate departments. For example, Mencap are assisted by the DHSS, while because of the nature of our charity we would have to apply to the Ministry of Education.

You should only apply for money for *specific* projects, and your application should be accompanied by your costings.

If the cap fits

If you are a small fund-raising organisation with a limited objective you won't need to concern yourself with things like covenants, major sponsorship deals or the finer points of investment. But for other, more long-term projects it is well worth exploring these opportunities of raising money. Once again, it is a question of getting someone in the know to advise you where necessary.

And if you think all this is rapidly turning you into a marketing manager, tax expert and investment specialist all in one – well, these days, that's the name of the fund-raising game.

10 · The End of the Story

Giving it all away

The purpose of fund-raising, of course, is to give it all away. But you'll find *that's* the really difficult part!

A one-off donation for a specific requirement is relatively simple – once you have reached your target you hand over the cheque. But when you're raising money for your charitable objectives it's difficult to give money away in a responsible and cost-effective manner year after year.

The main problem

Once the world hears about you, you will be bombarded with requests for grant-aid – free money is a popular thing! You must therefore have an organisation capable of handling the avalanche of requests for help. And it's here that you will recognise the value of having clear-cut charitable objectives.

The grants committee

The composition of this committee is very important. Above all, you need those with knowledge and skill to assess the merits and demerits of the hundreds of applications for grant-aid you will receive.

The chairman must be someone special – a highly respected name in the field in which you are dealing. That way, the public can be sure that the funds are in responsible hands.

The treasurer will obviously be a member of this committee. He or she has to keep your charity in the picture as to how much money there is to give away and how much is left in the kitty – an exercise not as easy as it sounds to achieve. The treasurer must be careful not to overspend.

The remainder of the grants committee can be made up from your most experienced members, including your past chairman.

Speaking from experience . . .

About 45 per cent of Lord's Taverners' funds go towards youth cricket for disadvantaged youngsters. Imagine the number of cricket clubs and schools there are in the country who would like some cash from our Foundation. My office staff could not cope with the bids, let alone assess the validity of the requests. So we have laid down the following procedure:

A local club wants to apply for some cricket equipment to start a colts side. First it has to apply to its local County Association, who in turn will forward the request with a specific recommendation to the National Cricket Association — the governing body of cricket outside the first-class game.

The secretary of the NCA will then collate all the requests from the forty-eight County Associations and appear, cap in hand, before our Foundation.

The procedure for giving away our 'NEW HORIZON' mini-buses is much the same:

My mini-bus secretary examines every request for a bus. Those requests that look appropriate will receive a questionnaire asking about anchor points for wheelchairs, the need for a rear-door lift and other technical points.

There is also the question of self-help. Wherever it's feasible, we ask for a degree of local fund-raising, and we make up the deficit. Our grants committee approves the bus programme on a quarterly basis, as with all other grants.

In addition to the above, our other principal beneficiary is the National Playing Fields Association which receives an annual sum from us for its play schemes.

To summarise . . .

1) Giving away money responsibly is more difficult than raising it.

2) Your charity workers and the public will be sensitive as to how and to whom you give the money away.

3) A universally respected chairman of your grants committee will

alleviate any concern that the money is in safe hands and given away responsibly.

4) You will need people with appropriate skills on your grants committee. They need the necessary technical knowledge to assess the validity of the requests.

5) Your treasurer must keep a tight rein upon expenditure and avoid overspending. A running total should be kept of money available for disbursements each quarter.

6) It is sometimes a good idea only to give grant-aid upon receipt of the invoice for the goods. You can then ensure that all the money has been spent on what it was intended for, as well as checking on the cost.

A final word

Running a national charity has been a great privilege and brought me much pleasure. For as well as helping to brighten the lives of those less fortunate than myself, I have met — and can now number among my friends — a wonderful assortment of men and women from all walks of life.

But those I really admire, and whom I call the unsung heroes, are the thousands of dedicated voluntary workers throughout the country who devote a large chunk of their lives to charity. Without them, fund-raising organisations simply could not exist.

As the world gets more and more materialistic, I hope the few words Linda Zeff and I have written in this book will encourage all those who work for charity in such a self-effacing manner to gird up their loins and face the Great British public with increased confidence.

Of one thing I am sure — the British are as generous-hearted as any bunch of people in the world. So go out and grab them!

Appendix

Other useful organisations

Throughout this book you will find names and addresses of organisations that can help charities and other fund-raising bodies deal with specific aspects of their work.

Here are some others that deal with general topics.

Institute of Charity Fund Raising Managers
ICFM Trust
14 Bloomsbury Square
London WC1A 2LP   **Tel: 01-831 7399**

Formed in 1863, this offers membership to individuals who serve as fund-raisers for charities or as fund-raising consultants, and who accept the Institute's code of practice.

Full members will have had ten years in the profession, and be managing a team. They will also be raising not less than £100,000 per annum at a sensible cost/income ratio. Membership fee is £25 p.a. There is also a form of Associate Membership.

All applicants to the ICFM need to be supported by referees, and election is at the discretion of the Executive Committee.

Directory of Social Change
Radius Works
Back Lane
London NW3 1HL   **Tel: 01-435 8171**

This produces a large selection of literature on most subjects relating to fund-raising.

Social Service Advertising Ltd
West End House
11 Hills Place
London W1R 2AS   Tel: 01-437 8146

This organisation specialises in charity clients as well as distributing profits to charity by covenant. They also prepare studies in charity subjects by request.

Charity Commission   (Northern Office)
St. Alban's House   Graeme House
57–60 Haymarket   Derby Square
London SW1Y 4QX   Liverpool L2 7SB

Tel: 01-210 3000   Tel: 051-227 3191

The official custodian for charities. Anyone who wishes to apply for charitable status must do so through either one of these offices.

About the Authors

Anthony Swainson OBE was born at Bexhill-on-Sea and educated at St Paul's School, Hammersmith, in West London. He joined the Navy as an ordinary seaman at the age of 19 and rose to the rank of Captain, serving on frigates, destroyers, cruisers and aircraft carriers along the way. On promotion to Commander, he graduated from the RAF Staff College at Bracknell and served in the Policy and Plans Division on the Paris-based staff of SACEUR – Supreme Allied Commander Europe. His final posting was as Head of the Naval Mission to Libya at the time of the Qaddafi Revolution – for his services there at a difficult time he was awarded the OBE.

Other highlights in a distinguished career include being mentioned in despatches during the D-Day Landings, carrying the King's Colour at the funeral of George VI, being an usher at Princess Margaret's wedding, and witnessing the first British test of a hydrogen bomb on Christmas Island in the late fifties.

Anthony Swainson joined The Lord's Taverners in 1972 as its Director, in which capacity he attends no less than 200 fund-raising occasions every year. For the past ten years he has also been Appeals Secretary for the League of Friends of Normansfield Hospital (chairman Sir Brian Rix) who raise money for victims of Down's Syndrome.

Linda Zeff is a freelance journalist and writer who contributes to a number of national newspapers and magazines on a wide range of consumer and general interest subjects.

Formerly Assistant Editor of the *Jewish Chronicle* Colour Magazine and Supplements, she also worked for many years on *Woman's Own*.

Her other books include *Jewish London* and *The Beauty Treatment Handbook*, both published by Piatkus.

Index